AL ARGO

I0488791

160 SUPER SALES SUCCESS TIPS

Sales Tips To Help You Double
or Triple Your Sales Fast

Ordering Information:
This title can be purchased in bulk for your sales organization. All
proceeds go to create
Positive Impact around the world
For more information contact argoglobal@gmail.com.

Publisher's Cataloging-in-Publication data
Argo, Al, 1970-*160 Super Sales Success Tips* / Al Argo
     p.cm.
ISBN: 978-1519777034
ISBN-13: 1519777035

1. Business & Economics   2. Sales & Selling   3. Personal Success
I. Al Argo II. Title

Printed In The United States of America

10   9   8   7   6   5   4   3   2   1

Praise for 160 Super Sales Success Tips

"Every person who desires to grow in their field must constantly fill their minds with new knowledge and reminders of what it takes to be tops in their profession. With sales, we must also perpetually fill our hearts with motivation to handle rejection and maintain perseverance. Al Argo's newest book, *160 Super Sales Success Tips* is a perfect compendium of sales secrets, trusted techniques and motivational how-tos. I highly recommend it to any person aspiring to reach the pinnacle in the sales profession."

MICHAEL PODOLINSKY, CSP,
Global Speaking Fellow
Author of 16 books including his latest,
Managing, Motivating, Maximizing Teams in Asia,
McGraw Hill Publishing
www.MichaelPodolinsky.com

"This book is a must-have and a must-read for professionals who want to be exceptional in the sales industry! It will give you the mindset, heart-set and skill-set to boost your confidence on a daily basis and revolutionise your sales career!"

ADRIAN DING
Motivational Speaker, TV Host & CEO,
Maximum Impact Philippines

"Every sales professional, new or veteran, should read and continue to reread Al Argo's *160 Super Sales Success Tips*. My sales have definitely increased since beginning reading it! Thanks Al!"

JOHN MILLS
Sales Executive, Timberline Homes

"Growing your business, doesn't take time … it takes Focus! *160 Super Sales Success Tips* is a must read book so you create a "laser focus strategy" to building relationships, while growing your sales and business empire!"

GARY NOWICKI
Enterprise Director, Outstand.com

"When it comes to offering insight, Al Argo nails it in his latest book. You will find numerous nuggets of truth that, if applied, will serve you well. This is a must have resource for your library."

NIKITA KOLOFF
Coach, Counsellor, Mentor, Speaker, Author

"Every person in a service business, like myself, or in direct sales, like many of my clients, should read and begin to immediately implement the tips found in Al Argo's *160 Super Sales Success Tips.*"

ADAM MORALES
CEO, Trinity Accounting

Dedicated to my dad, Robert R. Argo, Sr. (1929-2001) who taught me to sell, influence, enjoy life and make a "Positive Impact" for others!

Special thanks to Adrian and Shelly whose friendship, faith and family continue to inspire me.

Special thanks to Jack the Wack, Jiggy Jr. and Y101 who aired these sales tips daily in the order presented here.

Special thanks go to Sharon, Yen & Paul who helped edit this manuscript! Thanks for being part of our family.

Special thanks go to YOU for reading and implementing these ideas and making a world of difference for others!

TABLE OF CONTENTS

"People will curse whoever withholds grain,
but a blessing will come to whoever is selling."
       – PROVERBS 11:26 (INTERNATIONAL STANDARD VERSION)

"The door is never closed to an effective sales
professional."

       – RABBI DANIEL LAPIN

1 – Finish Strong!

My wish for you and all sales professionals reading this is simply that you:

FINISH STRONG … and that is the first Super Sales Success Tip for you!

FINISH STRONG!

Imagine you are an Olympic runner and you are winning the race, but you know that if you slow down, if you look behind, you may stumble and you may lose the race. If you are an Olympic athlete you'd never slow down – you'd be focusing on finishing strong!

Whether it's Tuesday, Thursday or Friday and whether this is the first day of the year or the last day of the sales month - FINISH STRONG!

All of us will soon be into another week and then on into another quarter of the year – FOCUS ON FINISHING STRONG!

When you are determined to FINISH STRONG, you can finish strong and you'll see your sales increasing each and every day!

FINISH STRONG today and every day of the year!

> "Begin with the end in mind."
> – STEPHEN COVEY

2 – Think Clients for Life!

Our thinking impacts our attitudes and actions, and our attitudes and actions directly impact our sales.

If we really want to increase our sales, increase our influence and increase our persuasion ability, we have to think clients for life!

Whatever business you are in, from real estate to retail and from the restaurant industry to the insurance business, we have to think clients for life.

Relationships matter!

Ethical sales, influence and persuasions rise and fall on relationships. To keep friends (and clients) for life, focus on:

- Following up – Whether people buy or don't buy, stay in contact and build relationships.
- Following through – Do what you say you will do!
- Think first of the interests of others – Add value to others by thinking first of their interests.

If you want to increase your sales, influence and persuasion, think clients for life.

When you and I think clients for life – we position ourselves to attract and retain clients for life.

"The fact is, everyone is in sales. Whatever area you work in, you do have clients and you do need to sell."

– JAY ABRAHAM

3 – Think and Pursue TOMA!

TOMA is the acronym for "Top of Mind Awareness."

When people have a need, want or desire that your product or service fulfills, do they AUTOMATICALLY think of you?

If not – how can you increase TOMA?

By increasing "Top of Mind Awareness," you will increase your sales and profit.

One of the world's best companies at creating "Top of Mind Awareness" is Coca-Cola. In fact, I was recently at Sacred Heart School, Ateneo de Cebu, and noticed hundreds of red chairs. As I sat in one, I noticed the Coca-Cola symbol on the back of each chair. This is just one example of how Coke pursues top of mind awareness. I am sure you have seen the Coca-Cola logo on billboards, scoreboards and maybe even skateboards.

Now, I'm not saying go buy chairs with your logo on it, but at some level, do what you can to increase TOMA.

You can increase your TOMA through:

- Strategic marketing and advertising/marketing (paid and non-paid)
- Personal sales calls
- Asking for referrals

Today I want you to think:

How can I increase Top of Mind Awareness for my prospects and my clients?

> "I attribute my success to this: I never gave or took any excuse."
>
> – FLORENCE NIGHTENGALE

4 – Ask the Right Questions

Today's Super Sales Success Tip is ask the right questions.
Questions can help us understand our clients':

- Needs
- Wants
- Desires and
- Fears

The answers are always in the questions we ask. As we learn the art and science of asking questions, we can see our sales double and triple between now and the end of the year.

1) OPEN-ENDED QUESTIONS – These questions are designed to get your client or prospect to open up. They might sound like, "Tell me about your greatest challenge." or "If you found the perfect solution, what would it look like?"

2) CLOSED QUESTIONS – These questions are used to solicit a "yes" or "no" response. An example would be, "Can you see the benefit of a product like this?"

3) LEADING QUESTIONS – These questions are used to lead your prospect or client to a "yes" decision. An example might be, "Would you rather start on Wednesday, or would Thursday be better?"

To help us really understand our clients, close the sale faster and increase our sales, simply seek to ask better questions. After asking, don't forget to listen to what your clients and prospects have to say!

"Life is an exciting business, and most exciting when it is lived for others."

– HELEN KELLER

5 – Be Coachable

The highest-paid athletes in the world, think Manny Pacquiao, Michael Jordan and Michael Phelps, ALL have coaches!

The same is true with the highest-paid executives and sales professionals – they ALL have coaches.

Be coachable and continue to learn and apply new things in your sales career.

Coaches:

- Help you do what you do even better.
- Help you win.
- Help you shorten your learning curve and
- Help you practice what needs practicing!

Keep reading books like this, find great mentors and coaches and keep your focus on personal and professional development, and success this year and forever will be yours!

> "A coach is someone who can give correction without causing resentment."
>
> – JOHN WOODEN

6 – Watch Your Language

The language you use and the words you write impact your closing ratio.

Our language must be:

- Pleasant
- Precise, and
- Persuasive.

For example, researchers have identified one word that when used correctly is proven to boost our closing ratio by 66%.

My question for you is, how much would you be willing to pay in order to increase your sales by 66%?

Well, congratulations! Buying this book brought you access to the one word that has been proven to help you boost your closing ratio by 66%.

Don't take it lightly – the one word can be found in Tip Number 101 of the book you are holding in your hand! You might want to skip ahead and read that tip because the words mentioned there really have been proven to help professionals increase their sales, influence & persuasion skill!

Seek to make your language, pleasant, precise and persuasive, and you'll be on your way to tripling your sales.

"Those who guard their mouths and their tongues keep themselves from calamity"

– PROVERBS 21:23

7 – Know why People Buy!

Men never buy hammers and women never buy makeup,, just to have these things lying around. Men and women both buy the things they do for a specific purpose and reason!

As professionals, we need to know why people buy.

There is definitely both an emotional issue and an expectation issue going on when you sell your product or service.

By seeking to understand both the emotions and expectations of our clients, we will be able to continue to meet their needs as well as the needs of other prospects.

To explore this topic more, skip ahead to Super Sales Success Tip 91 and read "The Five P's of Buying!"

Today's Super Sales Success Tip is: know WHY people buy!

"People don't buy for logical reasons. They buy for emotional reasons."

– ZIG ZIGLAR

8 – 3 Keys to Effective Sales Presentations

According to the latest research on selling, there are three keys to effective sales presentations.

Are you ready?

1) Knowledge – As sales professionals, our clients and prospects expect us to be the product or service expert. But even more importantly, they expect us to be extremely knowledgeable about their own company and their needs.

2) Trust – As Stephen M. R. Covey writes in his bestselling book *Business at the Speed of Trust*, trust is the critical factor in business and in sales. And last but not least:

3) Adaptability – Salespeople typically tend to focus on stories/pictures, but buyers desire for us to simply focus on the facts. Be adaptable to buyers' desires.

Your knowledge, trust factor and adaptability are the three critical areas for effective sales presentations. How are you doing in each of these three vital areas?

"Trust is the critical factor in business and in sales."

– STEPHEN M. R. COVEY

9 – Be a Painter

I have a sister-in-law, Janna, who is a gifted painter.

As sales professionals, we also have to become excellent painters.

We must paint our prospects into a more favorable future after they use our products or services. Get them to imagine how their life will improve after investing in our product or service.

Help your clients see the future – help them realize what a better outcome they will get after using your product or service.

Be a painter!

It takes vision. It takes practice. It takes creativity.

The key to being a good painter is:

1) You have to start – A masterpiece can never be finished without first being started. Make sure as soon as daylight comes, you are calling on prospects or otherwise working the business.

2) You have to focus – It takes great focus to paint and to paint well. It also takes great focus to sell and to sell well.

3) You have to have paint – Make sure that as a sales professional, you have the tools and resources that you need in order to get the job done.

Be a painter, and paint your prospects and clients into the masterpiece.

"Be a painter, and paint your prospects and clients into the masterpiece."

– Al Argo

10 – Speak Your Client's Buying Language!

Every client or prospect has his or her own unique "buying language."

Different from buying motives, the buying language is simply how the prospect or client likes to be approached.

Four major buying languages are:

1) Time – People with this language will enjoy lengthy conversation and time with you.

2) Affirmation – People with this language will enjoy you complimenting their own company, achievements, etc.

3) Gifts – People with this language will appreciate a small token of gratitude like a premium such as a mug with a logo, specialized chocolate, etc.

4) Service – People with this language will appreciate the entire conversation, and your follow-up actions, being centered on service and what you can DO for their company.

Again, these are four major buying languages, and when you speak these languages, your sales, influence and persuasion will increase exponentially.

TODAY, focus on speaking your client's buying language.

By the way, 'buying' languages are similar to the 'love' languages and you can read more about these languages in *The 5 Love Languages* by Gary Chapman. It's a great book for couples, romantics and anyone seeking to have better relationships at home or in their work life.

> "Every client or prospect has his or her own unique 'buying language.'"
>
> – AL ARGO

11 – Keep Your Goals Visible

There is an ancient Biblical verse that says 'write the vision and make it plain.'

To me, this is a reminder that you and I need to not only set goals, but we also need to write these goals down and place them in strategic places.

For example, I write down major goals on paper ("I will speak 36 times around the world this year" or "We will have 24 separate locations of Upward Sports leagues around Asia by June 2018") and place them where I will see them often but others (outside my family) won't see them at all.

Yours might be "I will sell 100% of my yearly quota by June 30th!" or any goal you really want to focus on and achieve.

This goal reminder is about the size of a note-card and can be placed:

- On your dashboard
- On your bathroom mirror or
- In your calendar or planner.

Additionally, you can also type several goals to pop up when you turn on your computer or phone.

Write down your sales goals and other big goals for the week, month and year, and keep it visible on a daily basis, and watch as your sales begin to soar even higher!

> "If you have built castles in the air, your work need not be lost; that is where they should be. Now put the foundations under them."
>
> – HENRY DAVID THOREAU

12 – Do a Dynamic Demo

I was walking through the mall recently and came across a kiosk that sells high-end phone cases. These cases are so good that if you drop your phone, the case is guaranteed to protect it.

I asked a few questions and then walked off – the salesperson made no attempt to sell, influence or persuade.

If this had been my kiosk, each salesperson would be required to give a dynamic demo – it's as simple as wrapping your phone in the case and dropping it so people can see the product really does work.

Whether you are selling phone cases, headphones, cars or computers, it is possible, and highly effective, to give dynamic demonstrations. Instead of just telling your prospects what your product or service can do, show them!

Actions always speak louder than words.

- If you are selling the world's greatest vacuum cleaner, make a mess and clean it up.

- If you are selling the best cell phone protector, wrap your phone in the case and drop it hard on the floor.

- If you are selling a fine automobile, let the prospect take it for a test drive.

- If you are selling advertising, do a great spec ad or sample radio commercial.

Whatever you are selling can be demoed at some level – it may take creativity, but that is why you have a job.

Products don't just sell themselves – they need you to demo them.

Do a dynamic demo in order to sell more products or services.

13 – Remember the Sales Equation

The sales equation simply says that:

$$ATTITUDE \times ACTION \times SKILL = SALES$$

If you want to improve your sales, simply get better in one of these areas. However, if you want to dramatically improve and double or even triple your sales, seek to get better in all three areas.

Your 'attitude x action x skill' really does equal your results and that is, after all, what we get paid for.

"Everything has its wonders, even darkness and silence, and I learn, whatever state I may be in, therein to be content."

– HELEN KELLER

14 – Go for the Record

A few years ago, Austrian skydiver Felix Baumgartner attempted to become the first person to break the sound barrier unaided by any outside object. He was initially hindered by the weather and had to stay prepared and mentally focused until he finally succeeded. I encourage you to find his amazing footage on the internet. I am sharing this with you to encourage you to:

Go for the Record!

Attempt great things in your sales and marketing career and watch, as over time, you will accomplish great things!

Records are meant to be broken!

- Seek to become the top sales performer in your company and industry.
- Seek to sell more today than ever before.
- Seek to call on more clients and close more deals than you have ever done in a single day.

Your Super Sales Success Tip is to GO FOR THE RECORD today!

> "Life is either a daring adventure or nothing at all."
> – HELEN KELLER

15 – Invest in Your Personal Growth

Today's Super Sales Success Tip is: Invest in your personal growth!

There is no way you can go far and break the record without first investing in your personal and professional growth.

There are numerous ways for you to grow and learn!

Invest in:

1) BOOKS – Reading or listening to motivational, inspirational & non-fiction books.
2) COACHING – Getting coaching, whether it is image coaching, sales coaching or personal development coaching.
3) MEETINGS – Attending high-value seminars and conferences is also a sure-fire way to grow your network while focusing on your personal and professional growth.
4) PODCASTS and ONLINE LEARNING – Apple University, Coursera.com and other websites and podcasts have opened up a brand new and fascinating way for you to continue your personal growth journey.

Invest in your personal growth and get set to break all the records!

> "You and I are the same today as we are going
> to be five years from now, except for two things,
> the people we meet and the books we read."
>
> – CHARLES "TREMENDOUS" JONES

16 – Be Thankful!

The Super Sales Success Tip of the day is: Be thankful!

As sales professionals, we need to always have an attitude of gratitude.

We need to be thankful for our life, our family, our health, our job, our opportunity, our clients, our prospects and yes, even our competition.

Express your gratitude to those who have helped you in any way.

Words of thanks, and especially cards of thanks, go a long way to help solidify relationships, build trust, keep TOMA and in general, let people know that you are someone whose intention is to truly serve through selling.

Write a thank-you card or pick up the phone right now and say "Thanks" to someone who deserves it!

> "Cultivate the habit of being grateful for every
> good thing that comes to you, and to give thanks
> continuously. And because all things have contrib-
> uted to your advancement, you should include all
> things in your gratitude."
>
> – RALPH WALDO EMERSON

17 – Repeat That

The Super Sales Success Tip of the day is: Repetition is the mother of all sales!

What I mean by that is, typically people need to hear about your product, service or message between 7 to 10 times before the message will even begin to stand out in their mind.

So if you call on someone this month, this week or even today and they say they have no need, no desire or no money – BUT you feel they are a prospect and not a suspect – make it a point to contact or go see them once a month for the next 8 to 12 months.

Don't be pushy, but build a relationship!

Remember, repetition is the mother of all sales.

Make sense? Should I repeat that?

Repetition is, it really is, the mother of all sales!

> "Repetition is the mother of learning, the father of action, which makes it the architect of accomplishment."
>
> – Zig Ziglar

18 – Practice Your Pitch

Your Super Sales Success Tip of the day is: Practice your pitch!

As I write this, in just a few minutes, the world will watch another presidential debate.

Virtually everyone agrees that the challenger won the first debate and it was pretty obvious the incumbent president did not fully prepare.

This time will be different, and both candidates should be ready. (I believe you should always be ready – but that's another tip for another day.)

The incumbent has spent three of the last seven days practicing at what is called a "debate camp" while the challenger and his team of advisers have been preparing at his home.

Whatever your product or service is, be reminded to practice your pitch just like those aspiring to lead the country do during election time.

Your Super Sales Success Tip is to practice your pitch!

> "Whatever your product or service is, be reminded to practice your pitch."
>
> – Al Argo

19 – Know Your Numbers

Yesterday, during the presidential debate, both candidates were spewing numbers left and right. As sales professionals, we must also realize that we must know the numbers.

How many prospects did you call on last week?

How many opportunities are you currently working on?

What is your projected goal for this quarter and how many clients do you need to develop in order to reach this goal?

Track especially the number of appointments, presentations and actual sales.

In business, everything rises and falls on sales – and sales rise and fall with the numbers.

When I sold books in college, I carried a small goal card with me where I tracked the number of prospects I saw, number of demos and sales I made, as well as the number of callbacks I had for the evening.

Know your numbers so you can really know how close you are to doubling or tripling your sales.

> "In business, everything rises and falls on sales
> – and sales rise and fall with the numbers."
>
> – AL ARGO

20 – Embrace Technology

Many of you may know my name, Al, is an acronym for "Always Learning." Today, though, I want to discuss it as an acronym for "Always Leveraging." We can leverage and increase our sales by embracing technology.

Apps can never replace personal relationships, but they can help your memory, your personal growth, and help you retain clients for life.

A few apps to check out include:

- Evernote: Lets you save all kinds of documents in your device.
- Sales Tracking Calendar by PipelinePro: Helps you save contact info and track your pipeline.
- CamCard Free: Allows you to save business cards and have the data saved in your contact info at the same time.
- Square: Free app that allows you to accept credit card payments for a flat fee.
- GoToMeeting: A great app that allows you to attend meetings or present a meeting while on the road or at the home office.
- Keynote: Just a nice way to carry presentations with you to share with a client over coffee or lunch. Keep 'em brief though. And last, but not least . . .
- Audible: My favorite app of all time, which allows me to download full-length and abridged audio non-fiction books to enhance my personal and professional development.

"I can do all things through Christ who strength-
ens me."

– PHILIPPIANS 4:13

21 – Keep Your Family First

The Super Sales Success Tip today is a bit different, but it is indeed very powerful advice and can, in fact, help you sell more over the course of your career.

The sales tip is simply, keep your family first!

As parents, you are indeed selling your children on how to behave and act in the future.

As a husband, or wife, your spouse can serve as a positive motivating force helping you to sell and achieve more.

The weekend is coming (even if today is Monday – the weekend will be here before you know it), so seek to spend some quality time with your children, your spouse and even your parents if they are around this weekend.

Great sales professionals around the world understand work/life balance and the importance of keeping your family a priority.

Keep your family first today and let them know how much you really love them, care for them, and will always provide for them through serving others while selling.

"If you raise your children to feel that they can accomplish any goal or task they decide upon, you will have succeeded as a parent and you will have given your children the greatest of all blessings."

– BRIAN TRACY

22 – Productive or Just Busy?

Every morning at exactly 10 a.m. my phone buzzes with a private alarm for my eyes only. As I look at it, I see the words, "Productive or just busy?"

This reminder has been on my phone for several years to remind me that my focus each day is not to be just "busy", but to build relationships and to get things done!

What is the most important thing that you need to accomplish today? I encourage you to write it down and work hard and smart, to get it done.

Selling is all about building relationships, solving problems, making proposals and closing deals – make sure today that you are focusing on the things that matter.

Make sure today that you are being productive and not just busy!

"Productivity is never an accident. It is always the result of a commitment to excellence, intelligent planning, and focused effort."

– PAUL J. MEYER

23 – Define Your Mission
Statement

Everywhere you go, you see companies defining and proudly displaying their mission statement. Oftentimes the puffery says absolutely nothing and then, every now and then, you will come across a mission statement that is succinct and to the point.

My challenge for you is to define what your mission and your purpose, really is. I am sure it has more to do with selling just for the sake of selling.

It most likely has to do with making a positive impact on your clients, your family and even your community.

Define, remember and pursue your mission!

> "When you discover your mission, you will feel its demand. It will fill you with enthusiasm and a burning desire to get to work on it."
>
> – W. Clement Stone

24 – Schedule Think Time

One key thing that truly productive and successful people do is to schedule and utilize think time.

This time is any undisturbed block of time set aside for you to ponder your most pressing issues, problems, challenges or clients.

Creative answers come to you when you think about and write about issues – so keep a pen and paper or device handy to write and record!

Think time can be either structured or unstructured, and that is what we will discuss over the next few Super Sales Success Tips.

Today's tip is to schedule and utilize think time!

> "Schedule and utilize think time!"
>
> – Al Argo

25 – Unstructured Think Time

As mentioned previously, great achievers practice think time. This time can be structured or unstructured. In unstructured think time, it's OK to let your mind wander, as long as you are recording where your thoughts take you.

You might end up writing and recording goals, to-do lists, potential prospects, quotes, stories, etc.

When you let your mind wander, when you let your heart dream in unstructured "think time" and, here is the key, when you write down what you are thinking about, you increase your potential by 1000 fold, and that, my friend, is a great way to increase your sales, your income and your potential!

Practice structured and unstructured think time, and we'll talk more about structured think time in the next Super Sales Success Tip.

"Let our advance worrying become advance thinking and planning."

– Winston Churchill

26 – Structured Think Time

As mentioned in the last couple of tips, great sales professionals practice think time!

Today, I want to go just a little deeper and talk about structured think time.

In this period of think time, you need to ask yourself specific questions and work on the answer.

I've personally used structured think time to:

- Identify high-value prospects
- Remember and record stories to be used in presentations
- Solve great challenges and problems
- Write down both short and long term goals, and
- In structured think time, I have created action plans to reach these goals.

These are some of the things I've done in think time – what YOU can do is unlimited.

Today is a great day to begin, if you haven't already. Why don't you schedule an hour for yourself to practice think time – and whether it's structured or unstructured you WILL be rewarded for your efforts.

> "Few people think more than two or three times a year. I have made an international reputation for myself by thinking once or twice a week."
>
> – GEORGE BERNARD SHAW

27 – Tune into WCIDT

Each and every day and each and every hour, tune into WCIDT.

This internal station is not 50 thousand watts like some radio stations, but it can possibly help you produce 50 thousand or even 100 thousand sales over the course of your career.

WCIDT is simply an acronym that asks:

WHAT CAN I DO TODAY?

What can I do today to create more sales?

What can I do today to reach my goals?

What can I do today to generate more income?

What can I do today to further my personal development journey?

We can't do everything every day, but we can do something. Tune into WCIDT and ask yourself, "What CAN I do today?"

> "Tune into WCIDT and ask yourself, 'What CAN I do today to accomplish my hopes, dream & goals?'"
>
> – AL ARGO

28 – Treat Objections as Questions

Sometimes, after we make a presentation, our prospect will come back with an objection.

They might say:

"Yes, but …"

"Yes, but I can't afford it …"

"Yes, but XYZ has a similar but cheaper product …"

"Yes, but I'm just not sure it's the right product for me …"

Treat these and all objections as QUESTIONS.

When someone gives you an objection, oftentimes they are NOT saying, "I don't want to buy." Rather, they are saying:

"I need just a little bit more info before I give you my hard-earned cash."

Treat all objections as questions, and politely give some more information.

Today's Super Sales Success Tip is: Treat all objections as questions!

"Treat all objections as questions, and politely give some more information."

– AL ARGO

29 – Use the Classic Phrase "Feel, Felt, Found!"

The previous Super Sales Success Tip was to treat all objections as questions. Now, I want to encourage you to use the classic phrase: "Feel, felt, found!"

Imagine you are selling energy-saving light bulbs, and someone says they simply don't have the money to buy your product or service. You might say:

"I understand how you feel; in fact, others have felt the same way, until they found out that by buying and using our light bulbs, they can actually save an average of 20% on their electric bill each month. Can you see why so many are so excited about buying our light bulbs? Even though they are a little bit more expensive up front, they really can save you money from the moment you begin to use them."

The Super Sales Success Tip of the day is to use the classic phrase: "Feel, Felt, Found!"

"The best and most beautiful things in the world cannot be seen or even touched - they must be felt with the heart."

– HELEN KELLER

30 – Reward Yourself!

Today's Super Sales Success Tip is: Reward yourself!

Work Hard – Sell Smart – Reward Yourself!

It might be a movie, a special meal, or a private beach weekend that gets you excited, but set high sales goals, work to achieve them, and when you accomplish your hopes and dreams, reward yourself!

Always remember:

"All work and no play makes for a dull day, but, all play and no 'sell' - only sets you up to fail!"

Between now and the end of the quarter or the end of the year, set a high and ambitious sales target and pick a way to reward yourself after you accomplish your sales goal – write it down, and then let me know about it. Really, I'd love to hear from you, and you can reach me at argoglobal@gmail.com!

> "All work and no play makes for a dull day, but all play and no 'sell' – only sets you up to fail!"
>
> – AL ARGO

31 – Believe in Yourself

Today's Super Sales Success Tip is: Believe in yourself!

It's extremely important that you and I are sold on ourselves.

This is not cockiness, but a quiet confidence.

If you do not believe in yourself, your sales will suffer.

If you do not believe in yourself, you need to sell yourself to yourself first.

How can you EVER sell anyone your product or service if you can't sell yourself to yourself?

Again, Henry Ford said, "Whether you think you can, or you think you can't, you're absolutely right."

Believe in your ability, believe in your future, believe in yourself and believe that today can be one of the best days of your life!

Today's Super Sales Success Tip is all about encouraging you to BELIEVE!

"Whether you think you can, or you think you can't, you're absolutely right."

– HENRY FORD

32 – Believe in Your Product or Service

Today's Super Sales Success Tip is to believe in your product or service!

The greatest sales professionals in the world always believe in their product or service.

You know you believe in your product or service if you use, consume and prefer your product over other brands.

Let me explain: If you are working for a BMW dealership, you'd better be driving a BMW.

If you are selling XYZ vacuum cleaners on straight commission, you'd be doing yourself a favor to have an XYZ vacuum cleaner at home.

If you are selling insurance, make sure your family is adequately insured with the insurance policies that you sell.

If you are asking for donations, you'd best be supporting the cause yourself!

Whatever your product or service is, make sure you believe, and I mean really believe, in your product or service.

Use it and prefer it, so you can refer it with honesty, enthusiasm and your good example.

Of course, if you are selling planes, helicopters or advertising you might not be able to rush out and buy whatever you're selling, but you can still believe in your product or service.

Remember, believe, really believe, in your product or service!

> "Use it and prefer it, so you can refer it with honesty, enthusiasm and your good example."
>
> – AL ARGO

33 – Stretch Yourself!

The Super Sales Success Tip of the day is: Stretch yourself!

Seek day in and day out to go beyond your perceived limits.

Records are still being broken and will continue to be broken.

If you determine that you can break them, if you determine that you can stretch yourself, you will become more successful than you have ever dreamed or imagined.

Set a big, ambitious goal and then take immediate action toward reaching that goal.

You might start with doubling the goal you have for yourself – that is an example of stretching yourself.

You might start by calling on the prospect you fear the most – that is an example of stretching yourself.

You might start by asking me to come consult with you or to address your group or company – that is an example of stretching your company.

I have found great success, motivation and reward by constantly taking the road less-traveled.

As three-time Olympic champion Gail Devers says, "Every accomplishment starts with the decision to try!"

Your Super Sales Success Tip of the day is: Stretch yourself!

> "Every accomplishment starts with the decision to try!"
>
> – GAIL DEVERS

34 – Invest in Yourself

Let's start by reviewing recent sales tips:

I recently encouraged you to REWARD YOURSELF.

Then I exhorted you to BELIEVE IN YOURSELF.

We talked about the importance of BELIEVING IN YOUR PRODUCT OR SERVICE.

And previously, the sales tip was simply to STRETCH YOURSELF.

Today's Super Sales Success Tip is to INVEST IN YOURSELF.

Before writing this, I have invested in my day by spending an hour exercising and walking.

Already today, I have also invested in my body by taking the absolute best vitamins, minerals and nutritional products available.

Already today, I have invested in my mind and future by reading a great non-fiction book by one of the world's greatest businessmen.

Of course, the things we read, take and do cost us time, money and energy, but SEE the time, money and energy as a wonderful investment into your future and potential.

INVEST IN YOUR LIFE, BECAUSE IT'S THE ONLY LIFE YOU HAVE on this earth.

Today's Super Sales Success Tip, again, is to invest in yourself.

"Invest in your life and future."

– AL ARGO

35 – Don't Ruin it for the Next Salesperson

The Super Sales Success Tip of the day is: Don't ruin it for the next salesperson.

You and I are simply not going to sell to everyone. How do you treat those who make the decision not to buy from you? We SHOULD treat them with the respect and friendliness with which we would treat our own best friend.

Unfortunately, this is not always the case.

Several years ago, I received a call from a cruise company with a very "special offer." As a person who dreams of my next cruise vacation, I listened with true interest and asked a few questions.

After about 15 minutes of phone conversation, I told the saleslady I was not going to buy from her. After trying to overcome my objections, she finally became rude, crude and very angry and said something to the effect of, "Thanks very much for wasting my time!"

My question for you is, "Do you think I would EVER buy anything from her or her 'cruise line' at any point in the future?"

Even when clients and prospects DON'T BUY, try to leave them laughing and definitely leave them feeling better for having talked to you!

The Super Sales Success Tip of the day is: Don't ruin it for the next salesperson!

"Even when clients and prospects DON'T BUY, try to leave them laughing and definitely leave them feeling better for having talked to you!"

– AL ARGO

36 – Go From Stress to Success

It's time to turn your stress into success!

While too much stress is a negative, moderate stress can serve to:

- Move you to action, and
- Serve as an aid to enthusiasm!

Here are four quick ways to turn stress into success in sales:

1) Focus on the FUNdamentals – Have fun on each sales call, and have fun prospecting and make selling a game!

2) Compete against yourself – Seek to break your own records. If the most you've ever sold is $100,000 worth of product or services a month, set your target on $250,000 next month.

3) Understand that a "no" is not a personal rejection. When your prospects or clients say "no", they are not rejecting you, and they may not even be rejecting your product or service, but in most cases they are saying, "I'm choosing not to buy today, but if you are friendly and pleasantly persistent, I just might buy from you in the future!"

4) Eat and exercise – Last but not least, get adequate exercise and eat a balanced diet with adequate fruits and vegetables while drinking lots of water throughout the day. Some research even indicates drinking water with lemons, limes or calamansi can also help prevent certain sickness and disease..

The Super Sales Success Tip of the day is turn your stress into success!

"The greatest weapon against stress is our ability to choose one thought over another."

– WILLIAM JAMES

37 – Pursue Your Passion!

One of the very first books I was tasked to read while beginning my MBA program was the book *"Passion and Purpose"* by Marlys Hanson and Merle E. Hanson.

On page 113, the Hansons write, "Nothing extra-ordinary is ever accomplished unless the work is performed by an individual who is 'motivated' to do that work."

My question for you today is: Are you motivated to do the work you are currently performing?

Do you have passion? Do you understand the purpose?

If you have the passion and understand the purpose, your sales will soar.

If you are lacking drive, passion and purpose, your sales will suffer.

If you can't truly get enthusiastic about what you are selling, you might want to consider doing something else.

BUT before you make that drastic decision, remember, the best way to become enthusiastic is simply to act enthusiastically!

The Super Sales Success Tip of the day is: Pursue your passion!

"Nothing extra-ordinary is ever accomplished unless the work is performed by an individual who is 'motivated' to do that work."

– M. HANSON

38 – Follow the Sale with Superior Service

Sometimes it's difficult to make the first sale, but it's even more difficult to make the second sale without superior customer service.

Make sure that your customer service is impeccable!

- Make sure your delivery, installation or training is completed promptly
- Answer the phone promptly and professionally
- Be quick to respond to email
- Handle complaints and concerns promptly

Remember again, a happy customer may not tell anyone, but an unhappy customer WILL tell everyone!

Your Super Sales Success Tip is: Follow the sale with superior customer service!

> "A happy customer may not tell anyone, but an unhappy customer WILL tell everyone!"
>
> – Al Argo

39 – A Quick Tip on Pricing

This is actually a topic I referred to in my book *Walking, Living, Learning!* Day 129 is entitled: "Pricing, Sales & Bringing in the Business."

The key with pricing is you can't set it too high and you can't set it too low. It's got to be just right.

Too high and no one will buy.

Too low and your business won't grow.

Your price point actually determines two things:

- Your position in the marketplace and,
- The profit for your company.

Brands like BMW and Mercedes are positioned as premium brands and are priced accordingly while the Mitsubishi Mirage is "marketed worldwide as a low-tech, low-cost, lightweight subcompact car" according to a recent article.

If you are creating a pricing strategy for your company, I would encourage you to consider having a line of products available. Make sure you have a low-cost (or entry level), a medium level, and a high-end model, product or service available! While a lot of product lines stop here and only have 3 price points I am encouraging you to go a step farther and create a premium end (or the top-of-the-line model) of the same product, service or offering!

Remember, your pricing determines two things:

- Your position in the marketplace, and
- Your profit for your company.

By the way, *Walking, Living, Learning!* covers all things personal and professional development, from leadership to marketing and from marriage to corporate communication. I think you'd enjoy it and find some great ideas (as well as discover some other great books) that can help you increase your revenue and results!

40 – Value Your Time and Your Client's Time

Time is money! Value your time and your client's time.

Let me give you a negative example. Last week, I ordered an international courier to pick up a small package to be sent to the USA. On the phone, I said, "Please bring exact change and an additional envelope."

At 4:15 p.m., when the courier finally arrived, I was shocked to discover he did not have change and did not have the envelope I had been promised.

He had to leave my office a2nd return the next day with an envelope – this wasted his time, his gas, my time and, worse, our office in the US was late getting the package.

For the last two months, this same courier company has been wasting my time by doing crazy things like this.

You have to realize in sales and service that customers may not have a choice today, but may have one tomorrow.

That is why FedEx, UPS and even LBC exist – to give this courier (whom I'm not naming) some good competition.

Value your time and your client's time, because if you waste too much of their time, it might give them a reason to shop around.

The Super Sales Success Tip of the day is: Value your time and your client's time!

"Don't evaluate everything, but evaluate everything that matters!"

– AL ARGO

41 – The 3 Focal Points of Great Leaders

Recently, I met Gus from Cebu, Philippines (now living in Las Vegas, Nevada). I was intrigued as Gus told me that he used to work in the very same department at GE with Jack Welch, long before Jack was made CEO.

On page 65 of his book *Winning*, Jack Welch says that great leaders focus on three things: 1) evaluating, 2) coaching and 3) building self-confidence.

Great CEOs, VPs, sales managers and sales professionals alike, all focus on these three things.

While we get paid only on results, these three activities can help us generate better sales results.

1) Evaluating: Evaluate the things that REALLY matter. Your sales calls, your speech, your closing procedure and your service. You don't need to evaluate everything, but evaluate everything that matters!

2) Coaching: If you are the sales manager, be a fantastic sales coach. If you are a sales professional, be your own sales coach. You can motivate yourself, encourage yourself and coach yourself to success. (That being said, it's also vital to listen, learn and apply lessons from others who are willing to coach you as well.)

3) Building Self-Confidence: How can you sell without confidence? Welch calls confidence the "fuel of winning teams" and says it is imparted through "encouragement, caring and recognition." Remember to praise your people publicly and correct them privately.

The Super Sales Success Tip of the day is to remember Welch's three focal points of great leaders: evaluate, coach and build self-confidence!

42 - Treat Each Customer Like They are the President

On page 26 of *Eat Mor Chikin: Inspire More People*, S. Truett Cathy encourages us to treat each customer that we have contact with as if they are the President. Assuming you like your president, this is great advice. But even if you don't like your current president, you should still treat him or her with dignity and great service and go the extra mile to please them and their entourage.

Cathy writes, "If you were working in a restaurant and suddenly the President ... showed up, your voice and facial expression would change. You'd be eager to serve the President well, make sure he had a clean table, then go up and see if everything was all right, or if he needed anything. If we're willing to do that for the President, why not treat every customer that well?"

Mr. Cathy, founder of one of my favorite American restaurants, Chick-fil-A, is absolutely right – we must treat each customer like we'd treat the President if we want people to continue to elect to do business with us!

The Super Sales Success Tip of the day is: Treat each customer like they are the President!

> "If you were working in a restaurant and suddenly the President ... showed up, your voice and facial expression would change. You'd be eager to serve the President well, make sure he had a clean table, then go up and see if everything was all right, or if he needed anything. If we're willing to do that for the President, why not treat every customer that well?"
>
> – S. TRUETT CATHY

43 – Cultivate Your Contacts

The Super Sales Success Tip of the day is: Cultivate your contacts.

Once at a three-day marketing workshop, I heard famed author Jay Abraham say, "The most underutilized asset in any business is relationships."

Abraham is right and, we should cultivate our contacts carefully, consciously and consistently.

1) Be Careful – Cultivate each relationship with care. The best way to do this is to truly think first of the interest of your contact. Never be pushy, never be arrogant, and never be clingy! Who would want a relationship with someone like that?

2) Be Conscious – Be conscious to retain contact information. Write down and follow through with any promises made by you and seek to consciously remember other relevant information about your contact.

3) Be Consistent – Be consistent in your follow-up. Write, email or text a thank-you after your meeting. Add your contact to your database and strive to reach out weekly or, at minimum, monthly, to each contact in your database.

Be careful, conscious and consistent as you seek to cultivate your contacts and grow your relationships and business.

The Super Sales Success Tip of the day is: Cultivate your contacts!

> "The most underutilized asset in any business is relationships."
>
> – JAY ABRAHAM

44 – Cultivate These Vital Sales Skills

My friend Gopi, from India, recently asked me, "What sales skills do you think are most important for success in sales?"

This is a great question and the answer is found in the ABC's of selling.

A – Attitude: Attitude is paramount to a successful career in sales. But as I say in the Super Sales Seminar and at other training events; "Attitude without action always leads to delusion."

B – Belief: Believe in yourself and your product or service. Without a strong belief, your sales will be weak.

C – Character: Trust is critical in sales, and the best way to maintain trust is simply to be a person of integrity and character.

D – Demonstration: You can't make a sale without being with prospects. Whether you are with them on the internet, on the phone, or in person, when you are with them, you must present a powerful demonstration of your product or service.

E – Enthusiasm: Enthusiasm sells! Get and stay enthusiastic over your future and your product or service.

F – Follow-Through: The fortune in sales is in the follow-through. Follow up fast, follow up frequently, follow up and follow through.

G – Goals: If you want to be successful in sales, set high and ambitious goals, and do something every day to reach those goals.

These are the ABC's to success in sales:

Attitude, Belief, Character, Demonstration, Enthusiasm, Follow-Through and Goals.

Your Super Sales Success Tip is simply to cultivate these vital sales skills!

> "Always do your best. What you plant now, you will harvest later."
>
> – OG MANDINO

45 – Remember, People Love to Buy but Still Hate to be Sold

The Super Sales Success Tip of the day is simply to remember that people love to buy, but they hate to be sold.

In his 1969 book titled *Success with People*, National Speakers Association founder, Cavett Roberts wrote, "People Love To Buy But They Hate To Be Sold."

Cavett is right, you know.

If you feel like someone has taken advantage of you, you might say, "I was sold a bill of goods." But if you feel like you got a great deal, you'd probably say, "Look what I just bought."

Four ways to help people buy:

1) Find out what people's hopes, dreams, goals and objectives are.

2) Figure out a way your product or service fits into their hopes, dreams, goals and objectives.

3) Communicate to them how your product or service fits into their hopes, dreams, goals and objectives.

4) Help them fulfill their hopes, dreams, goals and objectives.

Remember, people love to buy, but they still hate to be sold! Encourage people to buy from you today!

> "People love to buy but they hate to be sold."
>
> – Cavett Roberts

46 – Learn the Art of Promotion

P.T. Barnum understood promotion! He once said, "Tell 'em what you're going to tell 'em; Tell 'em; then, Tell 'em what you told 'em."

This is the spirit of promotion!

No, you don't have to always be talking about yourself or your product or service, but it is still appropriate to let people know what you do! Four quick ways to promote the product or service you sell:

1) Tell everyone you meet what you do, and find out what they do as well. Communicating, and selling, is still a two-way street.

2) Carry a business card – Leaving your business card with someone is like leaving them a small reminder of your meeting. It provides

them something to file and a way to contact you when wanted or needed. That being said, try to make the first contact after your initial meeting.

3) Speak - Speeches given to non-profit groups, such as Lions, Kiwanis or Civitan clubs, or associations groups such as ASTD (American Society for Training & Development) or NSA (National Speakers Association), can go a long way in filling your sales funnel by helping you generate new prospects.

4) Use social media - Make your Twitter, LinkedIn, Facebook, etc. profile distinctly about you, but be sure to mention your company and product or service!

Your Super Sales Success Tip of the day is: Learn the art of promotion!

"Tell 'em what you're going to tell 'em; Tell 'em; then, Tell 'em what you told 'em."

– P.T. Barnum

47 – Engage Thy Prospects

Several weeks ago, my good friend Manu and I went to purchase some additional basketball jerseys for our Philippines Upward Sports league.

We only needed a small order this initial season but what we never got around to saying to the first potential vendor was that while the order was small this time, it would get bigger and bigger each year as the league continued to roll out across Asia.

Before we could tell her that bit of information, she was on the phone with another person while ignoring us, even though we had already started a conversation and were sitting in her showroom. I can't make this up!

She never said "excuse me" or even acknowledged our presence after our initial contact – leaving us no choice but to walk out and seek another vendor.

She obviously was not the owner and had no concern for the business whatsoever – she violated the fundamental sales rule of "Engage thy prospect."

Just like a great marriage has an engagement period – a great sale should always have a period of engagement.

The Super Sales Success Tip of the day is: Engage thy prospects!

> "Just like a great marriage has an engagement period – a great sale should always have a period of engagement."
>
> – AL ARGO

48 – Remember AIDA!

I recently had a seminar attendee ask, "What are some best practices for engaging clients and prospects?"

To engage our prospects or clients, it pays to remember the classic advertising formula, AIDA.

Are you familiar with AIDA?

A – Attention: If you want to get the client's attention, you had better pay attention to the client. Don't get distracted, especially when sitting down with a prospective buyer or established client.

I – Interest: Without interest in your product or service, people are NOT going to buy from you. Remember, by truly being interested in others first, it opens the door for people to become interested in your product or service.

D – Desire: By arousing desire in a prospect, you are one step closer to a deal. Desire is achieved when people understand WIIFM (What's in it for me?).

A – Action: Engage your prospects by calling them to action. What specifically would you like to see your prospect doing? What is the desired action outcome?

Engage your clients by focusing on AIDA – Attention, Interest, Desire and Action.

"Keep your face to the sunshine and you cannot see a shadow."

– Helen Keller

49 – The Ultimate Sell

Over the weekend I attended the beautiful wedding of two of my good friends, Gopi and Marites. When Gopi (from India) met Marites (from the Philippines) he fell in love with her and had to start selling himself to her. Marites became Gopi's ultimate sell.

Who is your ultimate sell?

If you could sell your product or service to anyone – who would it be?

Dream big – write your dream down, and begin to pursue your ultimate sell today!

I am not just talking about your ideal client – I am talking about your dream client!

I would encourage you to write a large list – from 25-100 dream clients, depending on your industry and product.

Write down the names and contact information and then begin to do something monthly to woo these dream clients.

You can make the ultimate sell – but first, you have to identify who is the ultimate sell for you.

Identify, pursue and woo your ultimate client!

Like Gopi and Marites, once you make your ultimate sell, great service, sacrifice and commitment will assure that you live, love and work together forever!!!

Now go pursue your ultimate sell today!!!

"You can make the ultimate sell – but first, you have to identify who is the ultimate sell for you."

– Al Argo

50 – You Become Like Who You Hang Around

Recently on a medical outreach in Cebu, Philippines, I had the privilege of meeting up with some folks I'd never met from the US and Dominican Republic (DR).

After spending a good amount of time with them, I looked at one of the ladies from the Dominican Republic and said, "Hey, you don't happen to know a lady named Bonnie Clowers who lives in the DR, do you?"

Her face turned to shock, then amazement, as she said,

"That's my best friend in the DR!"

I too was shocked because I was kind of kidding but had been thinking, "This lady is acting a lot like Bonnie would be acting if she were here right now."

We went on to discover we had several friends in common but I could not escape the fact that she acted so much like our friend Bonnie.

The sales moral is we become like those we hang around with!

Hang around positive people who have a can-do attitude!

Hang around ethical people who would never do a dishonest or immoral deed.

Hang around people who are already successful or who are striving to become better than they are today.

Hang around happy people.

Hang around people who you'd like to be like!

If we become like those we hang around – you'd better hang around the best of the best of the best in your city or company.

Your Super Sales Success Tip of the day is: We become like those we hang around, so be careful who you hang around!

"The sales moral is we become like those we hang around with."

– AL ARGO

51 – Build Rapport

The following three tips will help you establish rapport quickly and consistently.

1) Be in the moment. If you are there, be there! Pay attention to the one you are with. No one wants to do business with an aloof salesperson. The best way to be in the moment is to focus, concentrate and really listen.

2) Use the name of your prospect or client. – The sweetest sound in their ear is their name. Use their name often and correctly when talking to them.

3) Use the phrase, "Tell me about…" "Tell me about yourself." "Tell me about your company." "Tell me about your situation." "Tell me about your desired outcome."

The simple phrase, "Tell me about…" can yield tremendous amounts of information that can help you make and solidify the sale.

Build rapport with your prospects and clients by being in the moment, using their name and encouraging them to talk by using the phrase, "Tell me about …"

Email me at argoglobal@gmail.com with your question or comment on these tips – after all, I really want to build rapport with you!

Your Super Sales Success Tip of the day is: Build rapport!

> "Without rapport it is near impossible to make a sale."
>
> – AL ARGO

52 – Go for the WIN

"WIN" is a brand new sales acronym I am encouraging you to pursue. Go for the win by seeking to help your client or prospect WIN.

The 'W' in win is WANT – What does your prospect or client really want? If they already want the OUTCOME your product or service provides, then you are well on your way to making the sell.

The 'I' in WIN is INTEREST – Is your client or prospect already interested in your product or a similar service? If there is no interest but you know that a need exists, how can you stimulate interest?

As Jeffrey Gitomer says, "If the customer says they're not interested, it means you're not interesting."

The 'N' in WIN is NEED – Need-based selling reigns supreme. Seek to identify and meet the needs of your prospects and clients.

Remember, people, a lot of people, need the product or service that you are selling.

Find those people, deliver your message and go for the WIN.

When people WANT your product,

When there is an INTEREST in your service,

And when there is a true NEED;

As long as you are helping meet those needs, then everyone wins (except your competition!).

"Life is simply a series of sales presentations!"

– AL ARGO

53 – How to Overcome the "I'm too busy to meet with you" Objection

You may have heard it once, or if you've been in sales long enough, you may have already heard it 1,000 times, "I'm just too busy to meet with you!"

Setting the appointment is a sell, just like asking for and getting the business is a sell. Life really is simply a series of sales presentations! Make a great pitch and you'll get the appointment! Make a bad pitch and you'll hear "I'm just too busy to meet with you!" To get the appointment, be friendly, be fun and be focused!

- Be friendly – There is an ancient Biblical proverb that says, "He that wins friends, must show himself friendly!" I would encourage you to read the classic book *How to Win Friends and Influence People* by Dale Carnegie for more great information on winning friends.

- Be fun – Business does not have to be boring. Seek to become interested at some level in what your prospects or clients are interested in. Suggest a meet-up for coffee, tea, golf or other fun activities.

▣ Be focused – The real question is what is in it for your client. Generate interest by sharing this while setting up the appointment. "What's in it for you is …"

As D. Forbes Ley writes in his 1984 book *The Best Seller*: "If you create enough interest, no prospect is too busy."

Overcome the "I'm too busy to meet with you" objection by being friendly, being fun and being focused on generating interest.

54 – Samples Still Sell

Have you ever heard of the "puppy-dog" close? Maybe, maybe not?

This is where you let an individual or a family take home a puppy-dog, and the next day they must return it, or buy it.

Well, nine times out of ten, you've just sold a puppy-dog.

Last night, while filling up my car with petrol, a man came up to my window and offered to sell me some mangosteens. I immediately said "no"; after all, who wants to buy fruit at a gas station?

He insisted and persisted and put his hands in my car and said, "Here, try one."

I tried it, and it was delicious.

We bargained a bit and I bought a kilo of his mangosteens.

A good friend of mine, Nikita, sells a liquid nutrition drink consisting of vitamins, 65 essential minerals, mangosteens and aloe. His technique is also to give people a free sample because people really can tell the difference between his all-natural formula and other synthetic formulations

(He's even offering a sample to you, wherever you are in the world - just send an email with the word SAMPLE to argoglobal@gmail.com and I will pass your request on)

There is a large US-based cosmetic company that is adamant about their reps giving samples.

Many large grocery-buying clubs located around the world also benefit from sampling.

Whether its dogs, fruit, vitamins, cosmetics, groceries or anything in between, it pays to remember that samples sell.

Your Super Sales Success Tip is: Samples still sell!

55 – Emulate

Your Super Sales Success Tip of the day is simply to emulate!

Some call it modeling, others call it imitating and you can also use the word emulating.

Just don't make it too obvious, or it might be irritating.

Emulating is the art of modeling your speaking style, tone of voice and even some mannerisms of your prospect or client in an effort to foster rapport.

For example, if your prospect is speaking slowly you might want to slow your speaking style down a bit.

If your client is direct and to the point, he also probably expects you to be direct and to the point.

If my friend or prospect has their legs crossed, often I will consciously, or sometimes unconsciously, cross my legs as a way to emulate them.

There are some things you don't ever want to emulate – for example, you should never emulate your prospect when he or she is crossing their arms.

"Why not?" you may wonder – and the answer is simple – crossing of the arms is often, but not always, a defensive signal indicating the person might be doubtful, uninterested or even closed to the information you are sharing.

Your Super Sales Success Tip is to emulate the prospect or client you are with in an effort to strengthen rapport with that person.

> "There is little success where there is little laughter."
>
> – ANDREW CARNEGIE

56 – Do a Time Audit

Time is ticking away! Are you wasting, spending or investing your time?

You can do a lot of things with time, but one thing is for sure – you can't get it back once it's gone!

How are you spending your time?

I would encourage you to give yourself a time audit for the next week.

A time audit is simply a way for you to track what you do with your precious minutes and hours.

The very act of doing a time audit can help you be more productive, because you really want to appear to be productive, disciplined and effective – even to yourself.

Check out our free sample of the Time Audit Sheet on Facebook at Super Sales Seminar and download your blank sample template today. Do this for today or the next couple of days, as I often do, and see what a difference it makes in your life.

You just might be surprised at how little time you are prospecting and selling and how much time you are doing low-value tasks.

Your Super Sales Success Tip is to download your free time audit sample and blank form at SUPER SALES SEMINAR on Facebook and DO a time audit for the next week!

P.S. While you are on Facebook, please like Super Sales Seminar as well. I often post similar sales tips there for your ongoing education and motivation!

"Make the most of every chance you get. These are desperate times!"

– Ephesians 5:16 (MSG)

57 – Establish Trust

Study after study has shown that buyers and clients want to do business with people they trust over anything else.

To build and maintain trust:

1) Think Relationships, not Revenue – It's the relationship that matters. Build the relationship, and the revenue will follow. If you are building relationships, you are first and foremost thinking of the interests of others, which leads you to …

2) Think WIIFT, not WIIFM – Think "What's in it for them," not "What's in it for me." When you think first about the interests of others, it will lead you to …

3) Be Honest Even When It Hurts – Well, if the product or service is not the best for your client, you'd need to tell them! If they'd be better off buying down the road, tell them. If they'd be better off waiting a week, tell them. If they need to go to another one of your own product lines – tell them. Be honest even when it hurts.

To build trust:

- Think relationships, not revenue.

- Think WIIFT, not WIIFM and

- Be honest even when it hurts.

When you do these three things, you'll be well on your way to doubling or even tripling your sales!

"Trust is a must unless you want to go bust!"

– Al Argo

58 – Be the Expert

People want to do business with people who really know what they are doing! Seek to be, or become, the expert in your chosen field.

If you are in the field, know the field. Be the expert!

For example, if you sell advertising – study advertising from all angles. Become the "go-to expert" in your community!

If you invest enough time, energy and discipline into your work, you can become an expert on any topic you desire.

Malcolm Gladwell, in his book *Outliers* states it takes an average of 10 years or 10,000 hours focused on any one skill or topic for anyone to become an expert on that topic. Anything that you choose, with enough effort and time, you can become an expert in. I've heard others state more recently that within a year, you can become an internationally recognized expert, due to the internet leveling the education and communication playing field.

The key is to study the product or service that you are selling so that day-by-day and in each and every way you are getting better and better!

Your Super Sales Success Tip is: Be or become the expert in your chosen field!

"If you are in the field, know the field. Be the expert!"

– AL ARGO

59 – The Sell is in the Details

Remember, the sell is in the details!

Let me explain. On my way home recently, I passed a posted sign with the message,

"Car for sale – 555-2222"

That's it! There was no description, no detail, no story and, I guarantee you, no sale.

At least, no sale as quick as would be possible with just a little thought and effort.

With a little thought and effort, the seller of this car could have stated: "2014 Mercedes for Sale!

- Low Miles/Fire Red Color
- Fully Loaded/Leather Interior
- 1 Owner
- All service records
- Moving – Must Sell!
- Call 555-2222 to see this beauty before it's gone!"

Which ad would pull faster? Of course, the one with the details.

In your sales presentations, advertising or marketing – talk about features, benefits and tell a story, no matter how brief.

"Moving – Must Sell!" is a story.

The sell is in the details – share the details and make the sell!

Your Super Sales Success Tip is the sell is in the details!

> "I long to accomplish a great and noble task, but it is my chief duty to accomplish small tasks as if they were great and noble."
>
> – HELEN KELLER

60 – Know the 3 WTD's

Success in selling comes down to doing small things consistently well. The following list contains three common elements of highly successful sales professionals! Focus on these WTD's to have Super Sales Success!

In sales, you must have all three of the following elements:

1) "Want to" – Desire! – Achievement, great achievement, first starts with a burning desire. What is your burning desire for this week, this quarter, this year?

2) "Will to" – Determination! – As I sometimes say, "Determination determines your destination." You must have the "want to" and the "will to" in order to be successful. Don't quit when things get tough.

3) "Work to" – Discipline! – Discipline is the key to success in selling. It's a word not very popular with many authors or sales coaches. It sounds hard, right? But living a disciplined life can lead to living the life of your dreams. In his book, *The Common Denominator of Success*, Albert Gray writes that "Successful people are successful because they are willing to do the things that unsuccessful people are not willing to do." This, my friend, takes discipline.

When you combine "want to", "will to" and "work to," there is absolutely nothing that you cannot achieve! Desire, Determination and Discipline ARE the building blocks to doubling or tripling your sales FAST!

"Successful people are successful because they are willing to do the things that unsuccessful people are not willing to do."

– ALBERT GRAY

61 – Get Organized

It's time to get and stay organized!

Organization is the key to optimization … optimization is the key to optimal income.

Disorganization leads to disarray.

Lack of communication, dropping the ball on follow-up and missed meetings are all symptoms of disorganization.

Here are three ways to maximize your organization:

- Hire a PA: A PA (personal assistant) or even VA (virtual assistant) is one key to your optimal productivity. My PA helps keep my schedule, maintains my database, does follow-up. Properly trained, your PA should become your "right-hand man" as the saying goes.

- Write Everything Down: I heard it once said that "the weakest ink is better than the best memory." We really should seek to write everything down. Any time we promise an email, a meeting in the future or a follow-up of any kind, we'd better write it down, and track it daily to make sure things get done!

- Read A Great Book On Organization – Two great books I will recommend are:

  1) *The Organized Executive* by Stephanie Winston and

  2) *Getting Things Done* by David Allen.

Your Super Sales Success Tip is: Get organized to optimize your income!

> "Organization is the key to optimization...
> optimization is the key to optimal income."
>
> – AL ARGO

62 – How Much is it?

How do you handle it when people ask for the price before you even have an appointment?

That is a great question and very common in the direct sales industry.

Of course, if someone calls your grocery store and asks how much a jar of Jif Peanut Butter is – give them the price. Or if they call your movie theater and say, "How much are tickets to the 2 o'clock show?" give them the price.

But, if they are asking about a high ticket or variable purchase (advertising, training or insurance for example), you really shouldn't answer the price question over the phone.

Remember, in direct sales, the phone is most often for selling the appointment and the appointment is for selling you and your product or service.

So if price comes up too quick on the phone, you might say, "Are you more concerned about price or more concerned about generating the results you are looking for?"

"The best way for me to help you generate results is to meet up to make sure we are a good fit, and to make sure I have all the info in order to give you the best quote possible – I'm available later today, or tomorrow. Which day works best for you?"

This does three things:

1) Establishes that you are selective in accepting your clients. This introduces "scarcity" into your selling activity. We want to make sure we are a "good fit."

2) Establishes you have their best interest in mind. You're saying, "I need to get all the info so I can give you the best price," and

3) Gives alternates of choice: Both today and tomorrow lead to an appointment with you – but you let them decide which day is best.

63 – Enhance Your Image – Enhance Your Sales

We all know that image is very important. To find out just how important, I asked my good friend, motivational speaker and image consultant Adrian Ding about his thoughts regarding the sales professional's image.

According to Adrian, your image not only builds your reputation – it can also be directly responsible for helping you build your business.

Therefore, he suggests three areas we should focus on to enhance our image:

1) Dress – Dress for success! We need to dress up according to what is appropriate in our industry. It's also probably better to be a little overdressed than a little underdressed. It's always professional to have our shoes shined and clothes pressed.

2) Grooming – Small things like fresh breath and clean nails are a prerequisite to sales success at any level. Other things like a nice haircut for men and modest makeup for women can also only help. If you want to know more, consult an image consultant near you or email Adrian at supersalesintensive @gmail.com.

3) Communication Skills – What you say and how you say it speaks volumes about people's perception of you. Seek to continually improve your speaking, writing and listening skills. After all, without communication there can be no persuasion, can there? A great way to boost your communication skills is at Toastmasters International – tell 'em I sent you!! :-) Really, tell 'em! It's a great organization.

Your Super Sales Success Tip for today is to enhance your image - enhance your sales; so dress up, look great and speak well!

64 – Be Confident

Your self-confidence is contagious, convincing and critical!

No one wants to buy from someone who is not really confident in themselves or their product. Don't be cocky, but be confident in yourself, and show this by dressing sharp and looking people in the eye when speaking. Be confident in your product or service, or sell something that you can be confident in!

Four ways to develop your self-confidence include:

- Think confidently! Think, "Everything is possible and I can, I will, I'm going to make a difference!"

- Act confidently! By simply standing straight and projecting your voice when you speak, you can exude confidence to others.
- Think about others! Confidence blooms when you put the focus on others and not yourself!
- Dress sharp! Let there be no doubt you are ready for the day!

In the book *The Magic of Thinking Big*, Dr. David J. Schwartz also outlines four additional tips to help anyone increase their confidence:

1) Become A Front Seater – Sit up front during training and events. Not only will it help you hear and see better, but distractions will be minimized and confidence will increase.

2) Make Eye Contact – A cultural issue in some parts of the world, but if appropriate, make eye contact when selling, negotiating and persuading.

3) Walk 25% Faster – Simply walking faster between meetings, to appointments and elsewhere helps improve confidence, according to Dr. Schwartz.

4) Speak Up During Discussions – Don't be shy! Listen up and, when appropriate, speak up!

Be confident in all you do! Be confident in yourself, your company, your product or service, your future and especially your intent to bring positive impact into the world.

Confidence breeds confidence, and confidence with preparation breeds success.

"Whether you think you can, or you think you can't – you're absolutely right!"

– HENRY FORD

65 – See Success Before You Achieve Success

Today's Super Sales Success Tip is all about vision.

Can you visualize yourself as the well-dressed, well-groomed, and well-spoken sales professional we spoke of earlier?

Can you visualize yourself as the most successful sales professional in your company or industry?

Again, Henry Ford said, "Whether you think you can, or you think you can't – you're absolutely right!"

When Ford's engineers came to him and said, "Sir, it's impossible!" he responded with, "Keep working!" He saw it before the engineers saw it – he saw it and hired people who he knew could get it done.

You also can get it done – you can accomplish your hopes, dreams and goals!

You can accomplish anything or become anyone in the next 12 months that you REALLY want to accomplish or become. The question is, what do you really want to accomplish and who do you really want to become?

There is an ancient Biblical proverb that says, "Without vision, the people perish!"

Don't let your sales suffer because of lack of vision.

Don't settle for mediocrity, because mediocrity is simply the best of the worst and the worst of the best.

Strive for success – see great success and you'll be well on your way to achieving great success!

"Where there is no vision, the people perish."

– Proverbs 29:18

66 – Options are not Optional

No one likes to be pinned down, do they? Everyone loves to feel like they have options.

If people like to feel like they have options, you and I would do well to make sure we give them plenty of options – does this make sense?

Today's Super Sales Success Tip is options are not optional!

The options we give are often alternates of choice:

A common alternate of choice is, "Would that be cash or credit card?"

Some other alternate of choice sentences might include:

- "Can I get you one, or would you prefer two?"
- "Would you like the white one or the black one?"

An alternate of choice combined with a scarcity element might sound like the following …

- "Would you like the four-door model, or would you like me to see if I can get you the two-door model?"
- And one last one, "Should I train your team to double their sales this month, or should we start next month?"

Options always ask the buyer to pick one of two or three buying choices.

You are assuming the sale and giving your prospect a choice at the same time.

Remember, options are not optional if you want to achieve Super Sales Success!

"Options are not optional if you want to triple your sales!"

– AL ARGO

67 – Think ARGO

"ARGO" is an acronym for many things, but today I want you to recognize ARGO as an acronym for "Accepting Responsibility for Goals, Growth & Outcomes."

The first key is accepting responsibility!

Sales offers great freedom, and with great freedom comes great responsibility.

Does that make sense?

So many unsuccessful people plod through life blaming the economy, the weather, their health or their lack of resources as the cause of their inability to be financially secure or even to make a sell.

It's simply not so, Joe!

Unsuccessful people can always find an excuse – successful people accept responsibility and FIND A WAY.

That way always has something to do with goals and growth.

You know I love to set high and ambitious goals, and I think you ought to set high and ambitious goals as well, but with all our goal-setting, don't forget to focus on your own personal and professional growth.

Without growth on your part, your goal-setting will be in vain.

With growth, your goal-setting will be like propane – igniting you faster and faster toward the success you seek.

Your goals and growth can lead to some amazing outcomes, and I'm encouraging you today to "Think ARGO," which is a reminder to "accept responsibility for your goals, growth and outcomes!"

> "Without growth on your part, your goal-setting will be in vain. With growth, your goal-setting will be like propane..."
>
> - AL ARGO

68 – See the Gatekeeper as a Goldmine

Selling is a relationship game, and you must be selling everyone you come into contact with, including the gatekeepers.

Gatekeepers are those people who serve as PA's, secretaries or administrative assistants to other people in authority who may actually purchase your product or service.

Their role is not to keep you from their boss – their role is to serve their boss, protect his or her time and make sure their boss has the resources he or she needs.

Your role is to see the gatekeeper as an ally and not as an adversary. Remember gatekeepers:

- Are people too, and should be dealt with respectfully and with dignity.
- Are full of information regarding your client or prospect, i.e. their likes, dislikes, habits and schedule.
- Are able to help you get in the door or make you stay out of the door.
- Are often able to influence a buying decision because of their words, tone of voice and hints regarding specific salespeople they come in contact with.

Your Super Sales Success Tip of the day is to see the gatekeeper as a goldmine!

"Character cannot be developed in ease and quiet. Only through experience of trial and suffering can the soul be strengthened, ambition inspired, and success achieved."

- Helen Keller

69 – Have Great Expectations

I've never read *Great Expectations* by Charles Dickens, but I love the title! If you are going to triple your sales, you need to have GREAT EXPECTATIONS!

Incredible results are simply the first-fruits of great expectations that have been combined with great faith and massive action!

What do you expect over the next six months? What do you expect over the next six days?

Expect greatness and you'll get greatness!

Why would you not expect this week to be the best week you've ever had?

Expect each day, week, month and year to be the absolute best, and day by day, in many different ways, you'll begin to get what you expect!

Expect to make the next sale! Expect the "yes!"

Expect to double or triple your sales!

Expect to double or triple your income!

Expect great things and receive great things!

Remember, with great expectations, great faith and massive action, anything is possible!

Today, I am encouraging you to expect great things this year and in the years to come!

> "Incredible results are simply the first-fruits of great expectations that have been combined with great faith and massive action!"
>
> – AL ARGO

70 – Wear This, Not That

What you say and what you wear both have an impact on the sales process. Would you ever buy an insurance policy from a guy dressed like a bum? Probably not!

Image does matter and a large part of image is the clothes we wear.

In his book *The E-Myth Revisited*, Michael E. Gerber cites a study that indicates exactly what colors "outsell" other colors.

So what color should we wear and what color should we avoid?

Gerber says that, all things being equal, wearing the color blue (think IBM blue) – like a crisp blue solid shirt or blouse, or even blue striped shirt will help you sell more.

That doesn't mean you need to change your corporate color or even wear blue every day, but when you have a sale you really want to make (and don't you want to make all of them?) – wearing blue might just be the extra edge that puts you over the top.

On the same note, Gerber indicates that we should avoid wearing brown. In my mind, this is especially true of brown shirts or tops and hopefully not so much on shoes or khakis, even though I've found my-self wearing khaki pants less and less since finding out this little bit of information.

The Super Sales Success Tip of the day is: Wear blue and not so much brown!

"Optimism is the faith that leads to achievement. Nothing can be done without hope and confidence."

– HELEN KELLER

71 – Take the Shortcut

Today's Super Sales Success Tip is: Take the shortcut!

Before you jump to the wrong conclusion, let me explain.

I am not saying cut down on quality; I am not saying cheat the customer; I am not saying do anything unethical or wrong. What I am saying is "Take the shortcut!"

My good friend, Pastor Rolando Turner, once named me "Shortcut Al" because he knew I was always looking for a shortcut to help me get from point A to point B faster.

What is wrong with that?

As long as I don't speed, go down a one-way street in the wrong direction or cut across a person's lawn, there is really nothing wrong with taking a shortcut, is there?

To take the shortcut, you must first know about the shortcut.

Step A is: "Find the shortcut!"

The best way to find the shortcut is to ask someone, but remember, sometimes they may give you wrong information, and that is why you have to test each shortcut for yourself. Does that make sense?

I see these 160 Super Sales Success Tips as a form of "shortcuts" for you and others in sales and marketing.

Step B is: "Take the shortcut!"

What good is knowing the shortcut without taking it?

Step C is: "Teach the shortcut!"

Remember, the teacher learns best – so teach what you know so you will earn best!

> "The teacher learns best – so teach what you know so you will earn best!"
>
> – AL ARGO

72 – Remember, Sales is a Transference of Feelings

In Zig Ziglar's book *Secrets of Closing the Sale*, he says that selling is nothing more than a "transference of feelings!"

Don't you agree with Zig?

"I love this product, and here's how it can help you as well."

"This is your current situation, and this is what I feel a good solution might be."

To maintain long-term integrity in sales, focus on the following three things:

- Be authentic – "If it's the right fit, let the client know; if not, let 'em know!" If the product or service is not the best fit, be quick to say, "This is not the best fit; I've thought about it, and you really should be looking at XYZ or ABC!"

- Be available - It's hard for you to transfer your feelings if you are not available. Be available! Maybe not 24/7, but how about 12/6? Be available for your clients and prospects.

- Be assuring - If you are convinced, it's much easier to be convincing. Your assurance, enthusiasm and contact make all the difference on the close ones.

The Super Sales Success Tip of the day is to remember that sales is a transference of feelings, so be authentic, be available and be assuring!

"Selling is essentially a transfer of feelings."

– ZIG ZIGLAR

73 – Take the "100 Call Challenge"

I once heard Brian Tracy mention how when he was first starting out, his main goal was to call on 100 prospects. He didn't worry about whether they bought or not – he just called on them as fast as he could. Because he really wasn't concerned about whether they bought or not, there was absolutely no pressure on them or him! This "no pressure" situation seemed to open the door for people to buy!

Whether you are starting out brand new, starting a new year or seeking to jump out of a sales slump, focus on the "100-call challenge".

Call on 100 prospects as quick as you can and see what great things happen!

Three tips for the 100-call challenge:

- Just make a decision to start
- Start today – with either your prospect list, calls or visits,
- Record each prospect or client you call on

The Super Sales Tip of the day is: Take the 100-call challenge!

> "Move out of your comfort zone. You can only grow if you are willing to feel awkward and uncomfortable when you try something new."
>
> – BRIAN TRACY

74 – Don't be Rude

I mentioned earlier about getting a call from a "cruise line" promoting a family holiday cruise. Never hearing about this cruise line, I immediately began searching for them online.

The salesperson even took me to the "port" site the cruise leaves from, but I went a step further and checked the name of the cruise line and resort on Google as well as the WHOIS information.

The reason I am saying this is you'd better believe your clients and prospects are checking you out online as well.

After asking a few more questions, I decided I did not need to buy the promotion at this time and when the salesperson realized I was not going to buy, she thanked me for "wasting her time."

I didn't say a whole lot, but I guarantee I will remember the name of her city, port and cruise line and will NEVER get on board that cruise.

Thank people for taking the time to listen, but don't get upset if they don't buy! Leave people with a great feeling about your company and never "close" the door on future sales by being rude to prospects.

"You don't close a sale, you open a relationship if you want to build a long-term, successful enterprise."

– PATRICIA FRIPP

75 – The Fortune is in the Follow-Through

About a year ago, I was filling in for my brother-in-law at his bowling league. My game was a little off the mark, as it had been a while since I had laced up the old bowling shoes.

His team knew me, and know I am open to coaching, so at the beginning of the second game, Mark came up to me and whispered, "Al, slow down and focus on the follow-through!"

I walked a few feet and another friend told me exactly the same thing: "Al, you have to focus on the follow-through!" I laughed as I told her that was exactly what Mark had just said.

I hit a strike on the very next throw – and raised my game score considerably by focusing on the follow-through.

The same message applies to sales.

Slow down and focus on the follow-through.

To put it another way, "The fortune is in the follow-up!"

Anyone can approach a prospect – once.

But it takes a real pro to build a relationship from scratch, and that is what sales is all about – building relationships, following up long term and meeting the needs of your clients and prospects.

Remember, the fortune is in the follow-through!

> "Anyone can approach a prospect once, but it takes a real pro to build a relationship from scratch."
>
> – Al Argo

76 – Don't be Afraid to Fail

In his 1985 book *Pushing Up People*, successful American businessman Art Williams says in business he sees four basic fears:

1) Fear of competition

2) Fear of controversy

3) Fear of what other people say and

4) Fear of things you can't control.

- Fear of Competition – You'll always have competition, at least if you are going for anything worthwhile. The key to competition is to focus on your own game and not on your competitor's game. Sure, we can learn from the competition, but we should never be intimidated by the competition.

- Fear of Controversy: Success always brings controversy. If you are doing anything worthwhile, expect the heat of controversy and press on through it.
- Fear of What Other People Say – Similar to controversy, many people are limited by others' beliefs and speech about them or to them. Don't believe lies others say about you – believe that you can do the impossible. Believe that you can achieve success. Believe that your results can double. Don't fear what other people say about you.
- Fear of Things You Can't Control – Well, someone taught me a long time ago you seek to change the things you can control and don't worry about the things you can't control. If you can't control it, why worry and why fear?

Another fear common in salespeople is the fear of the unknown. This fear has probably held more people back than any other fear combined. But like the other fears, it's just a self-limiting belief designed to keep you in the mud of mediocrity.

Have no fear – don't be afraid to fail, knowing that every failure is a stepping-stone to success.

Your Super Sales Success Tip of the day is: Don't be afraid to fail!

"The key to success is to focus our conscious mind on things we desire not things we fear."

– BRIAN TRACY

77 – Remember, Attitude is Important, But It's Not the Only Thing!

I will never forget walking with my wife in Singapore when we spotted a rather large-looking young man with a very tight-fitting "Attitude Is Everything" shirt on!

I looked at my wife and said, "Honey, if attitude is everything, that young man would likely be fit instead of flabby, don't you agree?"

You see, attitude is important, but attitude without action simply leads to delusion.

Even the Bible says, "Faith without works is dead!"

You can "name it," "claim it" or "proclaim it," but if you never plan, practice, prepare, stretch and then start the race, you'll never finish it, much less win it! Right?

That being said, I'm still encouraging you to have a positive, can-do attitude!

Three things to remember about attitude:

1) You are in charge and responsible for your own attitude! No one can force you to have a negative (or a positive) attitude! Don't let others' actions, habits or mannerisms make you lose your cool or composure.

2) Your attitudes are contagious to those around you! Often the attitude you encounter in others (especially those closest to you) is a mirror of your own attitudes. Your attitudes are contagious.

3) Your attitude can make or break a sell! I'm not sure if you hate to lose a sell, but it doesn't sound fun, does it? The sad thing is that a poor attitude is one reason why many sales are lost. The good news is a great attitude can help you close more deals, and close more deals faster, than a poor attitude.

You are in charge of your attitudes, your attitudes are contagious and your attitudes can help you close more deals!

Attitude is not the only thing – but it's an important thing!

"Inaction breeds doubt and fear. Action breeds confidence and courage. If you want to conquer fear, don't sit home and think about it. Go out and get busy."

– DALE CARNEGIE

78 – Get Enthusiastic

If you really want to double or triple your sales, get enthusiastic!

Enthusiasm sells!

Enthusiasm is contagious!

You don't have to be, and shouldn't be, obnoxious – but you should be enthusiastic.

According to Merriam-Webster enthusiasm means, "strong excitement about something: a strong feeling of active interest in something that you like or enjoy." The origins of enthusiasm come from Greek and actually mean to be inspired by God!

Get enthusiastic over your product, your service, your company, your community, your prospects and your clients!

My mentor and friend, the late Charlie "Tremendous" Jones, used to say that enthusiasm makes all the difference, and he was absolutely right – enthusiasm breeds results!

You must maintain and proclaim your enthusiasm for your career, your product, your service and your clients!

A great way to keep your enthusiasm up is to maintain a running list of the people, companies or organizations that have benefited from your product or service.

Show this list off to others and cite specific examples of how your product or service has brought positive impact to others.

"Success consists of going from failure to failure without loss of enthusiasm."

– WINSTON CHURCHILL

79 – Recognize that Everyone is Selling

I was speaking with Charlie "Tremendous" Jones at a large conference in Kuala Lumpur, Malaysia to a group of mixed professionals, when I asked the question, "How many of you are in sales?"

About 35 percent of the audience raised their hands. I continued saying, "Sales is not a title but simply influencing or persuading others to see things your way!" and I asked the question several more times until about 85 percent of the audience responded in the affirmative. Actually, a more accurate percentage would have been if 100 percent of the attendees had agreed. Don't you agree that we are ALL in sales?

To double your sales FAST, we must recognize that everyone is, in actuality, selling. Either you will sell your prospects and clients on you and your products or services, or they will sell you on the idea that they

1) Can't afford it

2) Don't need it or

3) Don't want your products or service.

The bottom line is, in every sales situation, someone is going to sell someone something!

Even in situations not typically seen as "sales" situations, a sell is often made!

The teacher must sell the students on learning.

The parent must sell the child on obedience.

The child sells the parents to get her a new toy.

The minister or priest must sell his congregation to take action on the message.

The politician must sell the voters on voting for him or her.

And the list really goes on and on!

Everyone sells something!

By the way, if everyone is selling, doesn't it make sense to boost your sales skill?

Recognize the fact that everyone is selling, and watch your own sales aptitude increase!

> "Life goes better for all of us when we learn to be givers and not takers."
>
> – RABBI DANIEL LAPIN

80 - Remember to Give

My mentor, Charlie "Tremendous" Jones, had Christmas 365 days a year at his home. To honor him, I wanted to remind you to remember to give whether it's even close to Christmas time or not!

Christmas is always a time of giving.

In Isaiah 9:6, the Old Testament prophesies the birth of Jesus when it says, "For unto us a child is born, unto us a Son is given…" (KJV)

Just as Christ was given to the world, and just as the wise men gave valuable gifts as they came to see Jesus, you and I have an opportunity on Christmas Day, and every day, to give valuable gifts to those we love, and we have an opportunity every day to give valuable gifts of service to those we serve.

As you spend time with your family, friends and clients, see your time as a gift. Be engaged, interested and involved with your children, friends, family and clients.

See your service as a gift to your prospects and clients. Give value first before asking for anything.

My #1 rule of business and life is: "Adding value brings positive impact!"

Make things better for your clients and prospects, and you'll be in business for life.

Christmas is not the only time for giving; today is a great day to give. Give to your family and friends, give to your clients and prospects, and give to your company or organization.

"Give, and it shall be given unto you ..."
— Luke 6:38

81 – Maintain Integrity

Character counts! Pivotal to your character is your authentic integrity. Be a man or woman of utmost integrity! Keep your word!

Say what you mean and mean what you say! Your word is your bond and helps your prospects and clients come to understand that your handshake and word is as good as gold.

Here are four Super Sales Success Tips to help you maintain integrity:

1) Don't over-promise: As a young teenager, I wrote a poem that I can still remember to this day.

   The title is "Willie Wont'he"

   "'Tis better to say 'I won't' – and don't,

   Than to say 'I will' – but won't!"

   Don't over-promise!

2) Keep your smallest promises! - Write everything down so you never forget what you've promised others you'll do! Fast follow-up is critical!

3) Keep your client's or prospect's best interest at heart: Don't sell just to make money for your company – sell because your prospect or client needs your product or service. When you sell out of the highest integrity – your referrals will skyrocket.

4) Never lie: It's simple but needs repeating: never lie and you'll always maintain your integrity!

When you do these four things, you will maintain your integrity and you will keep your clients for life!

> "Character is what you are in the dark."
> – DWIGHT L. MOODY

82 – Think Like You are "Self-Employed"

Whether you work for a large multi-national company or work for a small mom-and-pop establishment, think "I am self-employed!"

Whether you are on straight commission or not, think "I am self-employed!"

Care about your clients, your company and your community so much so that it is obvious you are going above and beyond the call of duty! This creates true positive impact and is a sure-fire path to increasing your sales.

When you think like you are self-employed, you'll:

- Work smarter! – We can all work hard, but to get ahead we, of course, need to work hard and work smart. It's easier said than done, but focusing on smart work can help you generate great outcomes!

- Waste less time, energy and resources! – Don't be "penny wise and pound foolish" as the saying goes, but we do need to utilize our time, energy and resources for maximum productivity.

- Want the best for the company and clients! – When we think like a self-employed person, we will genuinely want the very best for our company and clients. We'll understand that our success is dependent on their success and, most importantly, when you think "I am self-employed," you'll …
- Sell more goods and services! – You'll have the "If it's to be, it's up to me" attitude!

Think "I am self-employed" and stay on the path to doubling or tripling your sales fast!

83 – Be Empathetic

Put yourself in your client's or prospect's shoes!

As Stephen Covey says in *The Seven Habits of Highly Effective People*, "Seek first to understand, then to be understood."

I've heard it said that "sympathy" is feeling sorry that someone is going through something while "empathy" is feeling the very same emotion the other person is feeling.

Can you feel the "emotional" need, want or desire of your prospect?

What "emotional" pull would make them even consider you or your product or service?

What pain does your product or service alleviate?

What joy does your product or service bring?

What need does your product or service fulfill?

Think about others, put yourself in their shoes and sell to meet their needs, desires or demands! A great mantra to follow is to "wish for others what you wish for yourself" – this is empathy!

"Seek first to understand, then to be understood."

– STEPHEN COVEY

84 – Don't Shoot at Spiders

Like many people, my friend Cooter had a great fear of spiders. One day while in his bathroom, he noticed a small spider scurrying across the bathroom floor. I have no idea why his gun was in the bathroom, but according to his daughter, Ginger, he was so afraid of spiders that he grabbed his gun and began to shoot.

He didn't kill the spider, but he did leave a gaping hole in his bathroom floor.

The moral of the story is clear: Use appropriate action to get desired results.

Cooter did not achieve his desired results in this situation because he never used appropriate action. How much easier would it have been to step on the spider with a shoe, or to swat the spider with a newspaper?

I'm sure sometimes as sales professionals we, like Cooter, go overboard in our attempt to make a sale.

Unfortunately, our family had it happen to us not long ago. Leaving a mall in Asia, we were approached by a young man and lady encouraging us to visit their shop to claim a free gift. We had a few minutes to spare so we agreed to go visit. Once inside, we were greeted by six more sales agents who crowded around us, showing us a grandiose package we could "walk away with today."

- They ganged up on our family trying to persuade us to buy.
- In their excitement to sell, they got literally right into our face, and at one point someone actually spit on us – after this, would you have bought?
- They never established rapport – only focusing on their products and never on our needs, wants or desires!

Our goal is to sell, persuade and influence – when we accomplish this, we succeed, and to do this, we must use appropriate actions.

Remember, don't shoot at spiders, but use appropriate actions while selling.

"Anxiety does not empty tomorrow of its sorrows, but only empties today of its strength."

– CHARLES SPURGEON

85 – Script Your Script

Some companies have scripts that you can study and memorize and some do not. If your company has scripts already created, take them, learn from them and tailor them until they are "natural" for you and your nature.

If your company does not have pre-written scripts, then you will want to invest time immediately preparing scripts for the following:

Appointment setting call: If needed, this script can be written to help you briefly set up and qualify appointments over the phone.

Sales presentation: This script can help you sell over the phone or in person. The key is thinking it through and continually tweaking it based on what is working and what is not working.

Answering objections: The best time to answer objections is before they come up, so build some answers to common objections into your actual sales presentation.

Closing: Create or memorize several simple but powerful closing techniques. It might be as simple as, "It makes sense to me, what do you think?" or much more complex, but regardless, sales scripts presented naturally are effective at bringing in more business.

Remember, script your script in order to double or triple your sales fast!

"Expect the best. Prepare for the worst. Capitalize on what comes."

– ZIG ZIGLAR

86 – Create MADE to Stick Presentations!

A core action is your daily or weekly presentation to your prospects and clients. Seek to maximize each presentation through careful and creative planning.

I heard Dianna Booher once say that if you follow the MADE acronym in each presentation you give, you'll have most of your presentations MADE!

- Message – Know the core message you want and need to present.
- Action – What is the main action step you want your prospect or client to make?
- Details – Without overwhelming your client, what details should you share to make your case?
- Evidence – What testimonials, brochures, facts and figures can you present or even leave behind as evidence to support your presentation?

I am also going to encourage you to remember the Three-Prong Presentation Plan:

Three-Prong Presentation Plan

There are three main parts to all successful sales presentations:

- Problem: If you don't already know the problem, you'd better un-cover it before you continue. Uncover problems by asking questions, seeking to understand the company, situation or family and gathering information.
- Promise: The promise includes your recommended solution. What would you recommend if you were in the buyer's shoes? "Mrs. Prospect, if you do this, then I promise you that!"
- Proof: Persuasion is in the proof! Use testimonials, referrals and names to provide concrete proof.

Remember, to create MADE to stick presentations, you need to know the problem and offer proof regarding your promise, and MADE stands for your 1) message, 2) desired action steps, 3) details and 4) evidence.

"When one door closes, another opens, but we often look so long and so regretfully upon the closed door that we do not see the one which has opened for us."

– ALEXANDER GRAHAM BELL

87 – Remember, Prospects are Waiting For Your Recommendation!

Recently, I was talking to my good friend Mike Moody, who told me about selling his home in south Alabama.

He mentioned that his first real estate agent never gave him specific advice or recommendations about selling the house. For months and months the home was listed, and he'd ask if they should do this or that and she just never had an opinion on anything, even on the selling price.

Eventually, the Moody's decided to list with another agent and the new agent immediately made concrete recommendations about putting in new carpet and painting all rooms in a common neutral color. After making these changes, Mike received two offers on his home and sold the house within a week!

If you really want to double or triple your sales FAST, be such an expert that you are able to make concrete, specific and solid recommendations for your clients and prospects.

- Be the expert so you are able to make recommendations.
- Be willing to make recommendations.
- Be able to explain your recommendations.

As you are able and willing to make solid and rational recommendations, then you really will see your sales skyrocket, and that is what you really want, isn't it?

"A business absolutely devoted to service will have only one worry about profits. They will be embarrassingly large."

– HENRY FORD

88 – Create a Prospect List

Zig Ziglar always taught; "The most important thing to sales success is prospecting!"

Prospecting of course is simply looking for additional potential clients and buyers. I really love this step in the sales process and took great satisfaction out of beating my competitors to new businesses in my community because I understood the power of 'Getting there first and getting there fast!"

To truly double or triple your sales, create a prospect list of potential people, companies or organizations that might be a good fit for your product or service – and then go see or contact them!

Lead generation is the key, and you should focus a specific part of each week on this vital activity.

Your prospect list can include:

- Referrals from prospects or clients
- People you've read about or heard about in the media
- Places you spot while driving around
- New industries you'd like to target

The key with your prospect list is it MUST be written down in either your laptop, smartphone or on paper such as a regular yellow type pad.

This list should never be static, with new prospects added often and prospects being added to your client list as they buy!

The lifeblood of sales is prospects, so make a prospect list and get to work!

"The most important thing to sales success is prospecting!"

– ZIG ZIGLAR

89 – Driving the CAR will Take You Far

If you really want to double or triple your sales, focus on the CAR acronym I created some years ago.

C – CLIENTS – Seek and get more clients! Of course we want new clients! We wouldn't be in business long if we didn't, right? Clients come from building and expanding our relationships!

A – AMOUNT – With every client (or prospect), you ask yourself, how can I upsell, cross-sell or possibly (to avoid going away without any sell) downsell? Really focus in on asking, "How can we get a greater amount per sale?" The A in CAR is Amount.

R – REPEAT ORDERS – The R is simply a reminder to get even more repeat orders. So not only do we want more clients, but we want them to buy a greater amount and then we want to repeat the process quicker than ever before. How do we shorten the buying cycle? Can we make it two months? Can we make it one week? Can we make it three days? How can you do that? Asking this question forces your creativity! Analyze your clients and your prospect's wants, needs and desires.

R – REFERRALS – I added another R in CAR to make it CARR. The last R is simply Referrals. Ask for them. Get specific names and addresses or names and emails and follow up with each referral you receive. It's always easier to sell to a referral than to sell to a "cold prospect."

Remember to seek more clients, increase the amount per transaction, get more repeat business and ask for referrals, and you'll be well on your way to doubling your sales fast!

"If football taught me anything about business, it is that you win the game one play at a time."

– Fran Tarkenton

90 – Remember the SPCA Acronym

SPCA is simply an acronym I developed for the four possible types of people you may come across while selling.

In the USA, the SPCA is an acronym for Society for the Prevention of Cruelty to Animals, but in my acronym it stands for:

S – Suspects: People who are acquaintances but not really prospects! Beware because they can waste your time, energy and resources.

P – Prospects: People who could buy but haven't yet! Stay away from the suspects but invest in your prospects! Your focus is to move these people into your client list and on to the A-list!

C – Clients: Those whom you serve in one way or another! These might be internal or external clients. Keep their best interest at heart and soon you'll attract more clients!

A – Advocates: This is your A-list people (internal or external to your organization) who are really on your side and who go above and beyond the call of duty to refer people to you or promote you in some way, form or fashion. Recognize and reward your advocates publicly and privately!

Remember, most people you meet are either suspects, prospects, clients or advocates.

It's a jungle out there, so understand who is who and respond accordingly.

> "Selling to people who actually want to hear from you is more effective than interrupting strangers who don't."
>
> – SETH GODIN

91 – The 5 P's of Buying!

Our clients and prospects will buy from us for a variety of reasons, but often it will come down to one of the following five P's.

I call these the five P's of buying:

- To increase pleasure! – The person buys simply because they anticipate the pleasure that will come after getting the product or service. (Think recreational sports, beauty treatments, vacations, etc.)

- To increase productivity! – The buyer anticipates that things will get done faster and better! (Think vacuums, helicopters, office equipment, etc.)

- To make a profit! – The buyer believes financial resources will be saved or added to the bottom line! (Think investments, real estate, other merchandise, etc.)

- To support a purpose! – The person or company supports worthy causes to make a difference! (Think charities, causes, schools or religious institutions.)
- To resolve or prevent pain! – The person buys simply to cure or avoid potential pain. (Think insurance, auto clubs, nutritional products, etc.)

The more of the P's you can bring up in your presentation, the greater your potential for making the sale and doubling or tripling your sales! Remember, people always have a reason for taking or avoiding action, so you need to know why people buy!

> "Sell the benefit, not your company or the product. People buy results, not features."
>
> – Jay Abraham

92 – Know Why People Don't Buy

Just as you should know why people buy, you should also know why people might not buy from you! Six major reasons include:

No Desire – Your role here is simply to see if you can uncover an innermost need or desire.

No Urgency – Your role is to show why it is to their benefit to buy now rather than later or never.

No Money – Your role is to show them ways that lack of money is not an obstacle to the sale. Help them discover OPM (other people's money) or creative financing options.

No Need – Your role again is to uncover need, or to move on if there is truly no need, want or desire!

No Understanding – Your role is to help them understand! Information leads to sales!

No Trust – Your role is to be trustworthy. That is the bottom line.

By knowing why people might buy and why they might not buy, you will be well on your way to generating new clients and keeping the clients you have for life!

> "Success is never final. Failure is never fatal. It is courage that counts."
>
> – WINSTON CHURCHILL

93 – The Prize is in the Prospecting

You can sell more of what you sell by becoming a great prospector. When I first began to sell display advertising, one of the things I loved the most was prospecting!

I had my list of clients I serviced every week, but I had been taught by my father and other mentors to always prospect for new business. There were always businesses opening, restaurants, banks, spas, car dealerships and bookstores.

Whether you sell advertising, insurance, real estate or supplements, you've got prospects who are just waiting for you to find them. They are looking for you and they need you! If they want you, shouldn't you look for them so you can help them?

You should always be alert, asking and aligning!

1) Alert – Be alert for new opportunities and new businesses. Watch the emails coming into your inbox and the mail coming to your mailbox for potential prospects! As you ride through town or read through the paper, don't restrain from prospecting!

2) Asking – Ask every client who they can refer you to. Send emails giving and asking for referrals. Ask every person who does not buy who they can refer you to. Ask anyone! I've met prospects and clients at chamber meetings, church and check-out lines at the grocery store. Ask for a meeting, ask for a referral – just ask!

3) Aligning – Seek to separate from the suspects but align with the prospects. You might identify a prospect today but only be able to contact them tomorrow or next week. Align them in your CRM system, notes or phone so you don't forget them!

If you want the prize, you've got to prospect, so always be alert, asking and aligning!

94 – Seek to Negotiate Win-Win Agreements

David Lim, who led the first Singaporean team up Mount Everest, once said that if you had to pick one area to focus on to become more professional, it should be negotiation strategy.

Negotiation is simply the process of working toward a mutual agreement.

The key is to work toward a win-win situation and not a win-lose or a lose-lose situation.

In the book *Getting To Yes*, the authors, Roger Fisher, William Ury and Bruce Patton, emphasize the importance of:

- People: Focus on the people involved – not just the problem at hand.

- Interests: Seek common interest so you have common ground.

- Options: Create many scenarios, options and alternatives for the situation, and

- Criteria: Have specific criteria for the solution.

After your prospect has made a final "no" decision, there can still be hope. Ask, "What could we have done in order to strike a deal?" Often, this might bring life back to the table.

We'd do well to remember the words of John F. Kennedy, who said, "Let us never negotiate out of fear but let us never fear to negotiate."

Your Super Sales Success Tip of the day is: Seek to negotiate win-win agreements!

> "Let us never negotiate out of fear but let us never fear to negotiate."
>
> – John F. Kennedy

95 – 5 Keys to Persuading Others

The following five keys can be utilized to start the ignition of your persuasion power:

1) Be Convinced Yourself

It should go without saying that if you are not convinced, it's impossible for you to be convincing!

2) Tell a Great Story & Tie It into the Point

People want to know "What's In It For Me?" To help them understand, tell them a true story of how you or your product or service made a positive difference for someone else. If you are just starting out, ask your manager or peers for stories and testimonials to share.

3) Stick to the Facts and Nothing But the Facts

If it is 95 percent effective, say it is 95 percent effective. If there is a 60 percent on time rating, don't claim an 85 percent rating. Be honest! Don't exaggerate claims or mislead your clients or prospects in any way.

4) Ask For the Commitment

Many sales professionals are convinced, they tell a great story and they might even stick to the facts, but they fail in asking for the commitment. We must ask for the business! Ask and you shall receive! The absolute worst thing that can happen is you might hear a "no," but that is exactly what you will hear if you don't ask.

5) If You Get a "No" – See It As If They Just Need To "Know" More

If you do get a "no," you have to see it as your prospect just needing to know more! Obviously they do not have all the information you do, or they would say "yes!" Isn't that right?

When you get a "no," you can tell a new story and reiterate or make a new point. Give new information that can help the prospect go from a "no" to an "I know enough, so the answer is yes!"

Be pleasantly persistent during this persuasion process, and you really will be able to double or triple your sales fast!

"If it doesn't sell, it isn't creative"

– DAVID OGILVY

96 – Get CREATIVE

To boost your sales, boost your creativity!

In order to boost your creativity, simply follow the CREATIVE acronym I developed several years ago.

The C.R.E.A.T.I.V.E. Acronym

C – CAPTURE Creative Moments of Genius (via pen, paper, phone, camera, recording, note, napkin) – Don't let ideas slip away.

R – REVIEW Ideas Often – Have a creative file so you can review your ideas, hopes, dreams, goals often.

E – EXPECT Bursts of Creativity. You get what you expect! Expect creativity.

A – ACTIVITY Breeds Creativity. Showers, walking, writing, driving, cycling all can help bring forth your creative juices.

T – TAKE Think Time – Creativity can also be found in scheduled quiet time. Solitude is simply terrific at breeding creativity.

I – INVEST In Yourself – Creativity flows from personal development! Invest heavily into your brain!

V – VISUALIZE During Creative Moments – See the success you are seeking!

E – EXPERIMENT – Try New Things – As long as it is legal and ethical, why not? New experiences, travel, food, flavors, etc. can only help you enhance your creativity.

Selling requires creativity – so boost your creativity today and every day! There's tremendous power in this chapter, so it's wise to reread this Super Sales Success Tip and begin to apply the CREATIVE acronym!

97 – Think You Can!

Do you really want to double or triple your sales? I believe you can if you think you can!

This poem, written before most of us were born, is still a great inspiration!

"The Victor"
aka, "The Man Who Thinks He Can"
by C. W. Longenecker

"If you think you are beaten, you are.
If you think you dare not, you don't.
If you like to win but think you can't,
It's almost a cinch you won't.
If you think you'll lose, you're lost.
For out in the world we find
Success begins with a fellow's will. It's all in the state of mind.
If you think you are out-classed, you are. You've got to think high to rise.

You've got to be sure of your-self before You can
ever win the prize.
Life's battles don't always go To the stronger or
faster man.
But sooner or later, the man who wins
Is the man who thinks he can."

The Super Sales Success Tip of the day is believe in your skill, future
and ability! Think you can and you will!

98 – Write Down Your Goals!

Some of the strongest advice I can give you is to write down your goals!
Several years ago I wrote this poem that says it all about goal setting!

"Write Down Your Goals!"
by Al Argo

"IF you don't write your goal down on paper,
Beware, it may try to be an escaper.
But when you do write your goal in your journal,
What you have done is planted a kernel.
And everyone who knows anything knows,
That what a man reaps is what a man sows!
So write down your hopes and journal your goals
And press on through the highs and the lows.
Through the thick and through the thin,
If you never, never quit – eventually you win.
In every failure is a seed of success,
So keep trying, keep trying –
And you'll be the best.
Write down your goals
And surprise the rest."

This poem has been used to motivate students from Australia to
America and it's helped motivate salespeople from the Philippines to

Phnom Penh. I trust that it helps you motivate yourself to write down your goals in a clear, concise and specific manner. Do it now! What do you have to lose?

99 – Stay Off the Lazy River

I'm currently spending several days after Christmas at a resort owned by our friends in Mactan, Philippines, in an effort to spend quality time with my family and get some writing done as well.

I'd written 18 tips earlier this morning, so after breakfast I took a break and joined my children at the water park here.

After going down several wet and wild water slides with my family, I wanted to relax so we all got on the Lazy River. I think we had gone around several times when it hit me – many salespeople are not successful because they are also on the proverbial lazy river.

They are going around and around, taking it easy, relaxing and not focused or in any manner concerned with increasing sales.

I have a friend, Bill Billions, who is an actor, acting coach and owner of Hollywood Huntsville. He ends each of his emails with the words, "Get to work!"

I'm encouraging you with these same words: "Get to work!"

Get to work on your attitudes, actions, relationships, resources, goals, personal growth and development.

Get to work identifying your obstacles and embracing your opportunities.

Get to work for your company and your clients.

Get to work for your family, your future and for the future of your community and country!

Stay off the lazy river – GET TO WORK!

"Get to work!"

– BILL BILLIONS

100 – Get Social

We are living in the most connected generation in the history of the world. Social media, when used correctly, is great PR!

The Super Sales Success Tip of the day is: Get social!

Facebook, LinkedIn and Twitter are three platforms that can help you connect with others, build a reputation, build relationships and build your business.

Connect with others – Connect with your friends, acquaintances, co-workers and those you've just met for the first time.

Build a reputation – Add value before you ever even expect to build your business.

Build relationships – Have a good mix of personal and professional information. People love to see real people online. Keep it real and not just business related (and not just personal either!).

Build your business – Let people know what you are working on, including projects, events, new products, etc. Reach out to those who you desire to serve just as you would in person.

Use Facebook, LinkedIn and Twitter to connect with others, build a reputation, build relationship and build your business.

Your Super Sales Success Tip of the day is to GET SOCIAL!

"Become the person who would attract the results you seek."

– Jim Cathcart

101 – Understand the Power of Your Words

The following three words and phrases can be especially useful in helping you achieve Super Sales Success!

Use the word:

"YOU" – Quite possibly the most powerful word in the English language! Use "you", "your" and "yours"! I've used this to increase my open rate for emails and closing rate for sales. Use the contact's name close to "you" to make this word even more powerful!

"FREE" – This is possibly the most powerful word in advertising and marketing. Who doesn't like to get something of value for free! Use this word often and liberally to increase sales.

"BECAUSE" – This is possibly the most powerful word in closing sales. Research shows that those who 1) make a request, 2) use the word BECAUSE and 3) follow it with a reasonable explanation increase their closing rate by 66 percent! That is amazing, isn't it?

Lastly, use the phrase:

"Obviously you have a reason for saying that; do you mind if I ask what it is?"

Don't say "Why?" Ask, "Obviously you have a reason for saying that; do you mind if I ask what it is?" This acknowledges that the person's words are valuable while also allowing you to ask for an explanation.

Your words are powerful, so understand the power of the words you use!

> "Your words are powerful, so be conscious of the words you use!"
>
> – AL ARGO

102 – 3 Things to Remember

Here are three more things to remember that can help you double or triple your sales:

1) Be Aware of Your Obstacles but Focus on Your Opportunities – Obstacles are everywhere! Some within you or of your own devices and some external! Be aware of the obstacles (such as stress, time wasters or procrastination) and embrace each opportunity.

2) Never Quit – Never Give Up – If you set a goal to double or triple your sales and never quit, if you never give up, then you will achieve your goal. Success is never overnight, but it is attainable with time and persistence!

3) Commitment to Excellence – Excellence matters! You must be committed to excellence and you will achieve excellence!

Remember, "A good name is more desirable than great riches; to be esteemed is better than silver or gold." – Proverbs 22:1 (NIV)

If you are aware of potential pitfalls, embrace each opportunity, never quit and have an unwavering commitment to excellence then you can, and I do mean YOU, double or triple your sales based on the information you are reading and applying from this book!

Make it a great day and let me know how it's going every now and then! Contact me at argoglobal@gmail.com.

"Obstacles are necessary for success because in selling, as in all careers of importance, victory comes only after many struggles and countless defeats."

– Og Mandino

103 – Show Up!

Woody Allen said, "80 percent of success is showing up."

Your Super Sales Success Tip of the day is simply to show up!

To show up, you've got to get up and get at it.

This morning, it occurred to me again, that a man I've asked to help around our house has not been here in over five months even though I've asked him to come at least monthly. When we first moved here he designed and finished a huge, creative project but I've not seen him very much since.

You see, I know him, I like him and I trust him – but he's not showing up!

He is losing the business, and my home is somewhat suffering, because he is not showing up.

You've got to GET UP.

You've got to CALL UP.

You've got to SHOW UP.

If you don't do these things, your business will suffer, your clients and prospects will suffer and your income will suffer.

Remember the words of Woody Allen, "80 percent of success is showing up!"

"Eighty percent of success is showing up!"

– Woody Allen

104 – Win the Day – Today!

Wherever you are, be there! Napoleon Hill encouraged compartmental living in his classic book, *Think and Grow Rich*.

Today, your focus should be on getting the business – it should not be on what might happen this weekend or next month.

Your focus often determines what the outcome will be.

Focus on the one you are with!

Focus on their needs and objectives.

Focus on winning the business.

Focus on serving your prospects and clients.

Focus on the 4-8 actions that can make a tremendous difference in the bottom line.

In an earlier tip, I mentioned an acronym for WIN.

Here is another variation that can make a difference in helping you WIN your day:

W – WANT IT! – How bad do you REALLY want to win?

I – INVEST IN IT! – Are you committed to winning? Does it show by the hours you are investing? Does it shine through in your zeal and passion?

N – NEXT! – To win, you have to be aware of what's going on now, and also aware of what's next. What's next for you today?

You can WIN it, if you want it and work toward it with all your heart, mind and soul!

> "Do you want to know who you are? Don't ask.
> Act! Action will delineate and define you."
>
> – THOMAS JEFFERSON

105 – Be Honest

Recently, I went to the airport to pick up a friend of mine coming into Cebu, Philippines from Malaysia.

After picking him up, we talked about where to eat and we settled on going to Mang Inasal around Mango Square.

Several of us were together so we went in, ordered and sat down to wait for our food.

After we had finished our meal, a young lady came up to us and said, "I am so sorry, I accidentally overcharged your group. Here is 120 pesos back."

We were stunned.

We had not recognized being overcharged.

No one demanded money back – yet, here was a young employee at Mang Inasal who said, "Honesty is the best policy and I am going to do the right thing!"

I love it! The moral of the story is "Be honest, do the right thing and great things will come your way."

If you are ever around the Mango area in Cebu, Philippines, stop in at Mang Inasal and say,

"I read about you in Al Argo's *160 Super Sales Success Tips*!" The chicken is crazy good and the people are pretty good too!

> "In the modern world of business, it is useless to be a creative, original thinker unless you can also sell what you create."
>
> – DAVID OGILVY

106 – Selling in the Rain

I'm not sure where you are in the world today, but as I write this here in Cebu, Philippines, it is raining and it's pouring!

Today's Super Sales Success Tip is all about selling in the rain.

I was in my early 20's when I realized selling in the rain could be extremely lucrative.

Why?

Here are three reasons why today (and every rainy day) can be your best sales day ever:

- No one likes to sell in the rain, but successful people do what unsuccessful people are unwilling to do.
- Less competition – Hardly anyone gets out in the rain, so if you get out, you will be one of the very few going to see clients and prospects. When it rains, get out and go see more people than normal.
- Your prospects will know that you believe in your product or service. You would not be selling in the rain unless you REALLY believed in your product or service. Believe and go sell!

When it rains, go sell in the rain, and make it a great day!

"Don't watch the clock; do what it does. Keep going."

– SAM LEVENSON

107 – Identify and Implement Your Core Values!

Recently I finished reading a book entitled *Delivering Happiness* by Zappos.com CEO Tony Hsieh.

It's a great read for anyone in sales, leadership, small business or e-commerce.

One interesting observation is Tony's focus on the development of the Zappo's core values, which drives the company culture.

Starting with a list of about 50 possible values, they narrowed their list down to 10 core values including:

1) Deliver WOW through Service

2) Embrace and Drive Change

3) Create Fun and a Little Weirdness

I also formulated my own list about three years ago comprised of 13 values and character traits.

Mine include a focus on:

- Love
- Thinking first of the interests of others &
- Writing

The reason I chose 13 is because there are always 13 weeks in a quarter and 4 quarters in a year, so I spend one week a quarter focusing in on, learning about and implementing the particular value I am focused on for that week. Does that make sense? I learned about this while reading Benjamin Franklin's autobiography.

My challenge for you today is to think about, identify and begin to implement your own core values.

Write them down – and make a difference today and for the rest of your life!

Make it a great day!

108 – Deliver WOW Through Service

Have you ever had a WOW moment?

Have you ever had a WOW buying experience?

For the next few Super Sales Success Tips we are going to explore Zappos.com core values.

Today we'll talk about their first value, "Deliver WOW Through Service."

Zappos.com delivers WOW moments by giving every customer free shipping both ways as well as a generous 365-day money-back guarantee.

They have even been known to deliver flowers to their customers.

By the way, are you aware of what Zappos.com sells?

They sell shoes!

If an online shoe retailer can deliver flowers and deliver some amazing WOW moments for their customers and clients, what can you do in the company or organization you serve?

Make a focused effort to deliver WOW moments for your employees, customers, clients and prospects!

Please let me know how you deliver WOW moments by sending me an email at argoglobal@gmail.com.

In today's Super Sales Success Tip, I'm encouraging you to make today an amazing day for your clients, prospects, friends and family! Wow – they will love you!

109 – Embrace and Drive Change

For today's Super Sales Success Tip, we'll cover Zappos.com core value #2: "Embrace and Drive Change."

As sales professionals, when we ask people to buy, we are asking our clients and prospects to "Embrace and Drive Change."

So we'd also be wise to do the same in our own life and career! Makes sense, doesn't it?

Four ways to embrace change include:

1) Expect change! As Heraclitus said, "The only constant is change." Change is coming your way; it might be today, tomorrow or next week – it might be small or grandiose – but change is inevitable.

2) Ask yourself great questions such as "What's working?", "What's NOT working?" and "What can be improved?" Another great question is "What am I doing that I need to STOP doing?"

3) Be open to new ideas! And last but not least,

4) Be optimistic with regards to change! Change is a constant, so at least you and I should look for opportunities and seek to get the best out of everything that changes. You and I often get exactly what we focus on, so focus on the positive and you will find the positive in every situation.

Your Super Sales Success Tip of the day is: Embrace and drive change!

"The only constant is change."

– Heraclitus

110 – Create Fun and a Little Weirdness

I have a question for you!

"Are you having fun?"

For the next few Super Sales Success Tips, we are still digging a little deeper into Zappos.com core values.

I believe sales professionals around the world can learn from this billion-dollar company now owned by Amazon.

Zappos.com core value #3 is "Create Fun and a Little Weirdness."

If you are not having fun, well, you are missing out on something.

At Zappos.com you might sometimes find people dressed up like their favorite movie characters; sometimes you might even find a makeshift bowling alley in the middle of the call center or you can even take a class called "Pimp My PowerPoint." Do you see how they encourage fun and a little weirdness?

Our take away today is: Be unique – be YOU and be unique!

Don't try to imitate others – rather, try to stimulate yourself and others with a crazy sense of adventure, fun, excitement, innovation and enthusiasm.

This is what attracts customers and prospects to you!

Have fun and make a difference today.

Your Super Sales Success Tip of the day is: create fun and a little weirdness!

"Don't try to imitate others – rather, try to stimulate yourself and others with a crazy sense of adventure, fun, excitement, innovation and enthusiasm."

– AL ARGO

111 – Be Adventurous, Creative and Open-Minded

Zappos.com core value #4 is "Be Adventurous, Creative and Open-Minded."

Again, this makes for a great Super Sales Success Tip!

1) Be Adventurous – I've climbed mountains, jumped off mountains, jumped out of a plane, been whitewater rafting in Thailand, climbed a volcano in Bali and been massaged by an elephant in China (yes, it's true, an elephant massaged my back at the Yunnan Nationalities Village in Kunming, China) all in my thirst for adventure. Remember, even calling on new prospects requires a sense of adventure.

2) Be Creative – Creative thinking is the prerequisite for great problem solving. Hone your creativity by daily think time, working on puzzles or brainteasers or even drawing with the hand you are not used to writing with paper. Sometimes closing a high level prospect calls for a little creativity, so make sure you are stretching your creativity muscles!

3) Be Open-Minded – Remember, it's always good to stay open-minded so we can really understand how to meet the needs of our clients and prospects.

Your Super Sales Success Tip of the day is: Be adventurous, creative and open-minded!

"Creative thinking is the prerequisite for great problem solving."

– AL ARGO

112 – Pursue Growth and Learning

Again, for the next few Super Sales Success Tips, we will continue to explore Zappos.com core values.

We really can learn a lot from this billion-dollar e-commerce website. And core value #5 is "Pursue Growth and Learning."

I often tell people my name is AL and it's an acronym for "Always Learning!"

I will never forget seeing a bumper sticker on a professor's car in college that read:

"If You Think Education is Expensive, Look at the Price of Ignorance!"

We need to continually be pursuing growth and learning by:

- Reading books
- Listening to great podcasts/audiobooks
- Getting Coaching/Mentoring
- Attending Seminars/Training Events

Another great organization to be a part of for growth and learning is Toastmasters International.

This organization exists to foster communication and leadership development!

It's a great organization I have been a part of for years!

Hey, if you are already a part of Toastmasters, I'd love to hear from you how your chapter is doing and how you guys are progressing, so email me at argoglobal@gmail.com, and if you are not a member, go visit a club near you.

Your Super Sales Success Tip of the day is to pursue growth and learning!

> "If you think education is expensive, look at the price of ignorance."
>
> — ANONYMOUS

113 – Build Open and Honest Relationships with Communication

Zappos.com core Value #6 is "Build Open and Honest Relationships With Communication."

Your prospects, clients and colleagues desire communication.

In fact, recently the headlines in Zambia, a country in southern Africa, read,

"ZESCO should improve communication to members of the public over power outages."

This company has dropped the ball and now they are getting negative publicity.

Don't wait for negative press – make some positive changes today!

Here are three quick communication tips to help you build open and honest relationships with communication.

1) Foster the relationship – Dinner, coffee, questions, interest, even press releases can all help the relationship to grow.

2) Understand your objective – Have a clear purpose and focus on fulfilling that purpose.

3) Seek feedback – There is a fortune waiting in the feedback. Listen to your clients and customers and work to solve their problem and meet their need!

When you foster the relationship, understand your objective and seek feedback from others, you are well on your way to building open and honest relationships with communication.

114 – Build a Positive Team and Family Spirit

Zappos core value #7 is "Build a Positive Team and Family Spirit."

Your culture and surroundings are extremely important.

All things being equal, your customers and clients would rather buy from a company with a positive team and family spirit than from a company that devalues, humiliates and degrades their employees and suppliers.

Last Saturday, my children's school held their annual "Family Day!" This day was loads of fun for students, parents and staff.

Annually, other companies, schools and organizations also hold picnics, get-togethers, fun-runs and training events all in an effort to build a positive team and family spirit.

Make work fun, value your employees (and clients) and foster camaraderie to truly build a positive team and family spirit.

"I think togetherness is a very important ingredient to family life."

– BARBARA BUSH

115 – Do More with Less

Zappos.com core value #8 is "Do More with Less."

While Zappos.com is an American company, no one exemplifies this core value better than my friends in the Philippines, Indonesia and other developing countries.

Doing more with less is a true lifestyle when you get overseas.

"Recycling, reusing and reducing" is more than a mantra – it often means the difference between success and failure.

As sales professionals and leaders, we should also be aware that we can and should be doing more with less.

If we have less time, how can we utilize the time we do have more effectively?

If we have less resources, we have to maximize our creative thinking. If we have less clients, we have to spend more time prospecting.

We can do more with less, we just have to be focused on the outcome we desire.

Often we get what we desire, so focus and you just might get what you wish (and work) for!

Today's Super Sales Success Tip of the day is to do more with less!

> "Use it up, wear it out, make it do or do without."
>
> – ANONYMOUS

116 – Be Passionate and Determined

Zappos.com core value #9 and our Super Sales Success Tip of the day is:

"Be Passionate and Determined."

Charles M. Schwab once said that "a man can succeed at almost anything for which he has unlimited enthusiasm."

No matter what today holds, make a decision to be passionate, persistent and determined.

Your hopes, dreams and desires can come to pass when you work hard and smart!

I'll leave you with the words of Calvin Coolidge, who once said,

"Nothing in this world can take the place of persistence. Talent will not; nothing is more common than unsuccessful men with talent. Genius will not; unrewarded genius is almost a proverb. Education will not; the world is full of educated derelicts. Persistence and determination alone are omnipotent."

> "A man can succeed at almost anything for which he has unlimited enthusiasm."
>
> – CHARLES SCHWAB

117 – Be Humble

With this Super Sales Success Tip we'll wrap up our look at the 10 core values of Zappos.com.

I trust that you have enjoyed and benefited from our brief look at the corporate culture of what makes this great company work.

Core Value #10 is "Be Humble!"

In Proverbs 16:18 we read, "Pride goes before destruction, a haughty spirit before a fall."

I read a book several years ago called *How The Mighty Fall* by Jim Collins.

Jim Collins also says that sometimes companies or people fall because of "hubris."

Of course, "hubris" is just a fancy way to say "pride."

It might be OK to take pride in our work and do it to the best of our ability, but it's never OK to take pride in ourselves and talk about how great and mighty we are.

Whatever we are and whatever we've been able to accomplish, we are never "all that."

We have to remember to keep our eyes on the prize!

Keep our eyes on the mission and vision of why the company or organization even exists.

Of course, great companies and great individuals focus on consistently delivering value and positive impact to their clients and community they serve.

Stay away from pride – be humble – be real and make a difference!

> "Pride goes before destruction, a haughty spirit before a fall."
>
> – Proverbs 16:18

118 – Keep Planting Those Seeds

Sales is a continuous process. To keep reaping sales, we have to keep prospecting and planting seeds regarding our product or service.

Planting seeds might occur via sales calls, advertising, marketing or press releases.

It might occur online or offline, at chamber events, mixers or other business functions.

The interesting thing to note is all seeds fall on different types of ground, and you and I can't necessarily tell what type of ground our seeds will fall on.

For example, sometimes your sales may come from the most unlikely sources – so the saying is true, "You can't always tell a book from its cover."

The three types of ground our sales seeds fall on include:

Stony ground: These people may hear your message but have no need or interest in your product.

Good ground: These people will buy and invest in your product but may never share it with others.

Fertile ground: These people will buy and invest in your product or service and then spread the good news to their friends and family.

Your Super Sales Success Tip is to remind yourself to keep planting those sales seeds to keep reaping a sales harvest!

"Keep planting those sales seeds to keep reaping a sales harvest!"

– AL ARGO

119 – Ask for the Business

Today's Super Sales Success Tip is simple, yet fundamental!

You need to ask for the business!

Many new (and even some veteran) salespeople can set wonderful appointments, establish amazing rapport with prospects and even do dynamic demonstrations but fall short because they fail to ask for the business.

My friend, you have not because you ask not!

3 Tips For Asking For The Business Include:

1) Ask early – A single sale doesn't necessarily have to take all day! Ask for the business early and you might be surprised with a "yes, we'll take it!"

2) Ask confidently – Your confidence breeds confidence. Be confident in yourself and in your product or service! And last, but not least,

3) Ask expecting a "Yes!" – Be genuinely surprised if your prospect says "no!" Be surprised, but don't be unprepared.

Ladies and gentlemen, ask for the business today and every day! Ask early, ask confidently and ask expecting a "yes"!

"You miss 100% of the shots you don't take."

– WAYNE GRETZKY

120 – For Goodness' Sake, Establish Rapport

I received a call recently from someone trying to set an appointment with me.

He never asked me if it was a good time to talk, and in no way did he try to establish rapport.

Instead, he immediately said, "Jane Doe said you'd be interested…"

First of all, how can "Jane Doe" speak for me?

Does Jane Doe know all of my needs, hopes, dreams and priorities?

A better thing to say might have been, "Jane Doe said you might be interested…"

It is a small but very important difference when you are trying to establish rapport.

No matter how successful you are at sales – never forget the fundamental fact that without rapport, you can never have a true relationship.

And without a true relationship, you can never capitalize on the most important asset in sales, which is, of course, your relationships!

Remember, people still hate to be "sold," but they love to "buy," and they love to buy from people with whom they have rapport and a relationship.

Your Super Sales Success Tip of the day is: For goodness' sake, establish rapport!

"You can knock and get someone to the door, but to GET IN the door takes quick rapport! Establishing quick rapport is the key to getting in doors and getting into the hearts and minds of your prospects!"

– AL ARGO

121 – 4 More Ways to Establish Rapport

In our last Super Sales Success Tip, we talked about the importance of building rapport.

Now, let's discuss how to establish rapport.

First and foremost:

1) Be interested in your prospect or client – I've said it before, but it bears repeating: "If you want to be interesting, you must first be interested!"

2) Ask questions – Ask open-ended questions to get your prospect or client talking!

3) Look for common ground – A mutual friend, school, organization or even hobby can go a long way in helping you establish real rapport!

4) Make eye contact – Shifty eyes might appear to be a sign of a shifty conscience. Making confident but appropriate eye contact is a way to help you establish rapport.

These are just four more ways you and I can establish rapport. If you want even more ways to establish rapport plus much more personal and professional development content, please refer to my book, *Walking, Living, Learning!*

Make it a great sales day today!

"It's not about having the right opportunities. It's about handling the opportunities right."
– MARK HUNTER

122 – Have a Sense of Urgency

Today's Super Sales Success Tip is: Have a sense of urgency!

The clock is ticking, so you are either wasting or investing your time!

If it does not seem urgent to you, it will not seem urgent to your prospects or clients.

So today, and I do mean TODAY, cultivate a sense of urgency in your attitudes and actions.

Michael Hyatt, author of the book *Platform*, says, "More often than not, small companies have a sense of urgency. Why? Because their very survival is at stake. If they don't move quickly, they get squashed by larger, more established competitors."

He goes on to say, "The companies (and I would say the sales professionals) that thrive in today's economy will be those that can shift their cultures from the slower pace of business-as-usual to urgency."

Today I am encouraging you to have a strong sense of urgency!

Walk fast, respond quickly, do it right the first time and close that big sale NOW!

Do it now – tomorrow just might be too late!

"The companies that thrive in today's economy will be those that can shift their cultures from the slower pace of business-as-usual to urgency."
– MICHAEL HYATT

123 – The Incredible Power of Persistence

Persistence Pays! It's pure and simple and it's simply true.

I'll never forget my Dad's good friend the late great, Bryan Townsend, C.S.P., telling about how he called on one furniture dealer in Talladega, Alabama, for something like 15 years before the dealer finally bought anything from him!

A similar thing happened to the engineer who invented the airbag. He called on Detroit automakers for nearly 30 years before they embraced airbags.

Twenty-eight years after inventing the airbag, he sold not 1 million but over 20 million airbags to the auto industry for a net profit of over 110 million US dollars.

He didn't close the deal for almost 30 years!

But he didn't give up! Instead, he kept on keeping on!

Each day he heard a "No!" But he was eventually paid $15,000 in profit!!!!

My question for you today is, if you knew you'd eventually get paid on your efforts – would you persist until you succeed?

- Persistence pays off in selling and in life.
- Be persistent in making calls.
- Be pleasantly persistent while presenting.
- Be persistent while persuading.

Keep on keeping on and watch your sales double and even triple FAST!

"Persistence still pays!"

– AL ARGO

124 – Create a "To-Don't" List!

We've all spent time, often daily, creating "to-do" lists!

Today, I want to encourage you to also create a "to-don't" list.

These may be things you don't want to do today or ever.

You may even put things on your "to-don't" list that you are doing that you should not be doing – bad habits, time wasters, etc.

If you ARE doing things you don't need to be doing, write it on your "to-don't" list and then IGNORE IT or, if it needs to be done, DELEGATE it.

Michael Dell, founder of Dell Computers, once said, "Dell used to say, 'We're going to do everything,'" He then went on to say, "It's easy to say what you're going to do. The hard part is figuring out what you're not going to do."

Again, spend a little time today thinking about what you really do not or should not be doing.

Write it down and remember it so you can truly focus on the things you need to be doing.

Don't do what you should not do – do what you must, so that you can accomplish your dreams, desires and destiny!

Your Super Sales Success Tip for today is to create a "to-don't" list!

> "Don't do what you should not do; do what you must so that you can accomplish your dreams, desires and destiny!"
>
> – AL ARGO

125 – Adding Value

As sales professionals, our ultimate role is to add value to our prospects and clients.

I'm known around the world as "The Positive Impact Coach!" When I'm conducting seminars, trainings or speeches regarding leadership, sales or other topics I often ask my audience what their definition of positive impact really is.

I get many answers, but whether I am asking this question in Vietnam, Nepal, Malaysia, the Philippines or the USA, I, more often than not, get answers that can be summed up in my two-word definition: "adding value!"

Positive impact really is about adding value, which is what you do when you sell and deliver your needed product or service.

The respect, rapport and recognition you communicate also adds value.

The smile, skill and strategy you share with others adds value.

The time, thought and talent you give to others are even more ways of adding value.

Make a decision today to make a positive impact on your friends, family, prospects and clients!

Remember, you most always get what you go for, so go for greatness, go for positive impact, and go for adding value for others!

"Positive impact really is about adding value!"

– AL ARGO

126 – Don't Despise Small Beginnings

I was reminded recently of the Biblical verse found in Zechariah 4:10; "Do not despise these small beginnings…" (NLT)

This saying is an apt reminder for everyone in leadership and sales.

The biggest sale in the world could begin with a simple phone number and referral. It might seem small, but it's a great start.

You'll never know where it may go, unless you pursue it!

The biggest sale in the world could begin with a small, free sample.

Or the biggest sale in the world might just begin with a small, single purchase.

Taking care of the client or customer in this initial transaction often leads to bigger and more frequent purchases.

As you prove yourself trustworthy and proficient in small things, greater things will come your way.

Don't ever over-promise – instead, focus on over-delivering!

Your Super Sales Success Tip of the day is: Don't despise small beginnings!

> "A journey of a thousand miles begins with a single step."
>
> – Laozi

127 – Work on Your Message!

People buy, and don't buy, from you based on your message, or lack of it.

Your message is a fundamental focal point of your company, organization and every sales presentation.

Five tips to help you craft your message:

1) Begin in the beginning: What I mean is understand your product or services, features and benefits. You should also consider your company's core values when crafting your message.

2) Begin with the end in mind: What is your desired outcome after the message is delivered?

3) Consider your target market: To whom are you aiming to deliver your message? What are their demographics, their likes, dislikes, etc.? Know as much as you can regarding your target market.

4) Consider your delivery: Speaking to an audience of 1000 is different than delivering a message via radio. There is a place for both, but you have to understand the difference.

Presenting one-on-one is also different than selling to a committee. As you are crafting your message, make sure you consider your delivery.

Last but not least,

5) Craft a call-to-action: What good is delivering a message if there is no call-to-action?

What is your desired outcome? Do you want your prospect to sign an agreement? Call the number being promoted? Tell a friend about your website?

Be brief, clear and specific both in your message and call to action.

Today's Super Sales Success Tip is designed to encourage you to work on your message today!

Make it a great day as you continue to craft your message!

128 – Don't be Shy

Today's Super Sales Success Tip is: Don't be shy!

In my library, I have an original copy of the 1978 book: *Timid Salesmen Have Skinny Kids* by Judge Ziglar.

The premise of this book is set on helping you overcome fear.

FEAR is an acronym for "False Expectations Appearing Real."

Many people are paralyzed because of perceived fears.

My challenge for you today is don't let fear get in your way.

Don't be intimidated by your own thoughts; instead, overcome all fear with action!

Be bold and take massive action today!

Today is the first day of the rest of the sales week!

Today is your day!

You can if you think you can! Don't be shy in going for your hopes, dreams and aspirations.

After all, if you are bold, what is the worst thing that can happen?

You might get a "no!"
That's the worst thing!
Well, if you don't ask, if you are not bold, the answer is "no" anyway!
So go ahead, pursue your passion!
Be confident, be pleasantly persistent and pursue the business.
Your Super Sales Success Tip of the day is: Don't be shy!

> "Don't be shy in going for your hopes, dreams and aspirations!"
>
> – AL ARGO

129 – Event vs. Process

My question for you today is: "do you consider sales more of an event or more of a process?"

Think about that.

What do you say?

Event or Process?

If I had to guess, about 80% said "event" while 20% said "process."

After all, we've all seen signs that proclaim: "Sales Event of the Year!"

But have you ever seen a sign proclaiming "Sales Process of the Year!"?

Never!

Yet, I'm encouraging you today to think of sales more as a process rather than just an event.

An event is one-off. It's a moment in time. It happens once and it's over!

But if we see sales as a process, we understand it's a continuum.

As we maintain contact, customer service, follow-up and follow-through, we can truly generate clients for life.

The thing to understand about the sales process is that it really is a continuum. We're in it for the long haul. And last but not least, the process can always be improved.

Now, ask yourself, how can you improve the sales process you currently use?

> "You can't build a reputation on what you are going to do."
>
> – Henry Ford

130 – Constant Contact

Your Super Sales Success Tip of the day is: Stay in constant contact!

Communication is the key to relationships. Relationships are the key to sales success.

To foster your relationships, seek to stay in constant contact.

No, you don't have to contact every client or prospect every day, but you should strive to contact every client or prospect every month.

This is, of course, in addition to any other marketing efforts you already have in place.

To stay in constant contact, consider the following:

1) Create a database: As you meet people and collect business cards daily, add them to your CRM or database system.

    Is your database non-existent, stagnant or growing?

    If it's non-existent, begin it today by gathering all the business cards you have lying around and begin your database.

    If it's stagnant – begin to go to networking events at the chamber or other organizations.

    And if it's growing – keep up the good work!

2) Communicate with your database.

A database is no good unless you are reaching out to your friends, prospects and clients that are part of your database.

Send a personal e-mail or send a corporate newsletter to your database at least once a month.

After all, your list is one of the most valuable assets you have.

For true Super Sales Success, stay in constant contact!

"Fortune favors the bold."

– Virgil

131 – What Motivates You?

My question for you today is: "What motivates you?"

Researchers agree that people are motivated more by intrinsic needs and desires than by extrinsic motivating forces.

Three motivating factors I'll talk about today are:

- Power
- Prestige and
- Passion

POWER: People motivated by power are perceived to be dominant, confident and demanding. Sometimes they may even appear over-demanding.

PRESTIGE: People motivated by prestige are ambitious, focused and detail-oriented. Sometimes they may even appear to only be focused on high-end brands.

PASSION: People driven by passion are typically more social and are expressive, intuitive and often impulsive. Sometimes they may even appear to be overly enthusiastic.

Your sales team and your clients are motivated by different values. Power, Prestige and Passion are three, and we'll discuss three more in our next Super Sales Success Tip.

"The way to get started is to quit talking and begin doing."

– WALT DISNEY

132 – What Motivates You? (Part 2)

In the last tip, I asked the question, what motivates you?

Then we discussed how people are motivated by power, prestige and passion.

In this Super Sales Success Tip we'll discuss the motivating forces of:

- Profit
- Perfection and
- Purpose

PROFIT: In the last tip, we also talked about how people are often more motivated by intrinsic desires then extrinsic rewards.

That being said, some sales leaders are truly motivated by extrinsic rewards such as massive pay for themselves or profit for their company.

It's important that we recognize the motivating factors of our sales team because I have seen some companies not pay their sales champions well, leaving them open for recruitment from other competitors.

PERFECTION: Some of your sales team may be motivated by perfection. These people always splay by-the-book and are great at selling services such as tax services, accounting services, payroll administration. These people may not be as outgoing and energetic as others, but their expertise means they are highly trusted and are a valuable member of both your sales team and your client's team.

PURPOSE: Sales professionals motivated by purpose have a great sense of bringing value to the workplace. They understand that in their role and responsibility they can have a positive impact both for their companies and clients.

It's also important to note that sales professionals typically have a dominant motivating factor, but they also typically have one or two more secondary motivating factors as well.

133 – Use the Phone Wisely

This Super Sales Success Tip is all about using the phone wisely to make more sales.

Here are a couple of quick tips to boost your phone power:

Schedule your phone time! Schedule time for both outbound and inbound calls. This can greatly reduce you having to play "phone tag" with your prospects and clients.

If someone is not available, you should take the initiative to set a phone appointment with them.

Don't just say, "I'll call him back!" or "Have him call me!"

You can simply say, "I'll call Mr. Lee back tomorrow morning. 9 a.m. is convenient for me. Would that work for Mr. Lee, or should we make it 10 a.m.?"

If you're not available when someone calls you, have your assistant say something like, "He's not available – but he can return your call at 2 p.m. or 4 p.m., which is better for you?"

Be Brief.

Be Specific.

Be Polite.

Schedule your inbound/outbound calls, and

Set Appointments if you happen to miss your contact the first time.

When you utilize these tips, you will not only use the phone wisely but more importantly, you'll be on your way to doubling or tripling your sales.

"Motivation will almost always beat mere talent."

– N. R. Augustine

134 – Make People Feel Important

Today's Super Sales Success Tip of the day is to make people feel important!

I recently came across this quote by Mary Kay Ash, founder of Mary Kay Cosmetics.

She said, "Pretend that every single person you meet has a sign around his or her neck that says, 'Make me feel important.' Not only will you succeed in business, you will succeed in life."

When you look at people, see a VIP. Even if they are not a Very Important Prospect, they are still a Very Important Person, and you and I should help them feel their true worth!

Help people feel important!

Help people feel special!

Help people feel unique!

Today's Super Sales Success Tip of the day is simple, yet profound: Make people feel important!

> "Pretend that every single person you meet has a sign around his or her neck that says, 'Make me feel important.' Not only will you succeed in business, you will succeed in life."
>
> – MARY KAY ASH

135 – Start Early

Very early this morning as I was walking down the street I noticed two young boys, they were probably 5 or 6, selling Filipino sweets.

As they walked they were yelling, "Puto, Puto, Puto! Put, Put Put!"

The reason I am referring to them is that while most of my neighbors were still asleep, these two young boys had already began their day – selling.

This brings us to our today's Super Sales Success Tip: start early!

George Allen, Sr. once said, "Work hard, stay positive, and get up early. It's the best part of the day."

You may have also heard the saying, "The early bird gets the worm!"

There really is something about working hard and smart, in the morning, and all day long.

It's Labor Day as I am writing this here in the Philippines – so many will sleep late and take it easy all day.

But, I am encouraging you to get up early every day, get productive and make it a great day wherever you are in the world!

"The secret of getting ahead is getting started."

– MARK TWAIN

136 – Never Quit

Your Super Sales Success Tip of the day is: Never quit!

When I was just starting out in sales, I made a three-month summer commitment to sell in a city about 12 hours away from my hometown.

I was a long way from home.

I was there with my college buddies, but my family was nowhere around and it was straight commission and it was hot and people didn't know me and my car was having trouble and I was running low on money and I had about 1000 more reasons to quit… And after a week I decided that was exactly what I was going to do.

Thankfully, after a phone call to my father – he reminded me that if I had made a commitment, I really needed to keep it.

He told me, "Al, I am excited to see you, and I'll see you at the end of summer!"

In sales and in life, "If we never, never quit, eventually we win!"

Quitting is a bad habit we must do our best to avoid!

Press on, keep the faith, keep selling and you will be successful!

Remember, NEVER QUIT if you really want to double or triple your sales!

"If you never, never quit - eventually you win!"

– AL ARGO

137 – Focus

I heard a story recently of a police officer who practiced and practiced taking a gun from robbers and suspects. He would practice with his wife, his partner or anyone who would practice with him. He would retrieve the gun and then immediately give it back.

One night, he received a call to a robbery at a convenience store where he was able to use this maneuver for the first time in real life.

He and his partner walked down separate aisles to try to corner the suspect.

The officer was shocked when the gun-toting robber suddenly turned the corner – but the officer, because of his training – immediately grabbed the robber's gun. Amazing, right?

The robber was shocked when the officer immediately returned the gun to him!

Thankfully, the other officer walked up at that time and intervened so no harm was done.

As sales professionals we can be reminded of several things from this true story:

1) Practice: But understand, practice (perfect or not) makes permanent! In your practice, only do the things that you want to do in real life.

2) Stop: If, when practicing, the officer had stopped before returning the gun, he would have built a "trigger" (pun intended) into his actions so this event would not have happened. As sales professionals, sometimes we may also need to stop and observe what is really going on around us!

3) Focus: Unless you are intentionally winding down and chilling, it's always a good time to focus! As sales professionals and leaders – we need to focus on the ones we are with, focus on the task at hand and remember, focus on the big picture!

Your Super Sales Success Tip is focus!

> "Practice does not make perfect. Only perfect practice makes perfect."
>
> – VINCE LOMBARDI

138 – Check Your Attitude

Over the weekend, I had the oil changed in my vehicle.

As the service center finished changing the oil, they completed their work by checking the engine, tires, horn, etc.

This reminded me that as sales professionals and leaders, we need to check ourselves.

First and foremost, we need to check our attitude.

This is what Zig Ziglar called a "checkup from the neck up!"

I just want to share with you a quote from the Rev. Charles Swindoll;

"The longer I live, the more I realize the impact of attitude on life. Attitude, to me, is more important than facts. It is more important than the past, the education, the money, than circumstances, than failure, than successes, than what other people think or say or do. It is more important than appearance, giftedness or skill. It will make or break a company … a church … a home. The remarkable thing is we have a choice everyday regarding the attitude we will embrace for that day. We cannot change our past … we cannot change the fact that people will act in a certain way. We cannot change the inevitable. The only thing we can do is play on the one string we have, and that is our attitude. I am convinced that life is 10% what happens to me and 90% of how I react to it. And so it is with you. . . . we are in charge of our attitudes."

Ladies and gentlemen, as sales professionals check your attitude and make sure you are positive and productive today!

"A great attitude without great action only leads to great delusion!"

– Al Argo

139 – Check Your Actions

In the last Super Sales Success Tip we talked about the importance of checking your attitude.

Now, let's discuss checking your actions!

According to the Pareto principle, 20% of your actions produce 80% of your results and revenue.

The question is, what 20% of the things you do is most important and how can you do more of these things (thus improving your revenue and results)?

- Making the calls
- Setting appointments
- Doing presentations
- Writing proposals
- Being on the sales floor

VS.

- Being at the water cooler
- Taking a candy break
- Watching TV
- Gossiping

So, today's Super Sales Success Tip is: Check your actions!

What's working – what's not working?

What needs to be improved and what do you need to be doing more of?

As I always say, "A great attitude without great action only leads to great delusion!"

Get busy, stay productive and make it a great day today!

140 – It's Always Election Day

Somewhere in the world today it just might be Election Day.

But in sales, I am encouraging you to remember that every day is Election Day.

So you must ABC – Always Be Campaigning.

Here are several tips we can learn from the politicians:

1) Be on your best behavior – For better or for worse, most politicians are on their very best behavior during campaign season. You and I should be on our very best behavior all year long because it's always Election Day.

2) Focus on outcomes – People buy outcomes. Many politicians promise different and exciting outcomes if the people will just vote for them. As a sales professional, don't focus on features as much as you focus on benefits and outcomes!

3) Spread your message far and wide – Everywhere you look during elections, you see politicians campaigning. From in-person events to TV, radio and newspapers and even online! As a sales professional, seek to spread your message far and wide as well.

4) Honest and ethical incentives – Vote buying (a former common practice in the Philippines – and maybe other parts of the world) is illegal and should be stopped. But there are honest and legal ways to provide incentives. Maybe T-shirts, fans or other small premiums with your message are incentives.

For example, a popular gas station often has a tie-up with a soft drink company where for every fill-up of gasoline you get a free two-liter and for every oil change you get a nice premium hat and even a backpack if you use a certain brand of oil. Maybe, promises are incentives.

These are just a few things we can learn from politicians!

Remember, it's always Election Day!

> "Every waking moment we talk to ourselves about the things we experience. Our self-talk, the thoughts we communicate to ourselves, in turn control the way we feel and act."
>
> – JOHN LEMBO

141 – Talk to Yourself

Every year I read at least one book on how the brain works or on neuroscience.

Dr. Richard Restek, who wrote *Mozart's Brain* and the *Fighter Pilot*, and Dr. John Mendina, who wrote *Brain Rules*, are just two neurologists whose work I follow.

If you had the opportunity to talk to these or other neurologists, they would confirm the idea that as humans we are always talking to ourselves.

My challenge for you today, as leaders and sales professionals is – if we are going to talk to ourselves, let's go ahead and make it positive talk!

Go ahead – talk to yourself – but keep it positive.

Say things like:

"This is the best day ever!"

"I am the greatest salesperson in the world!"

"I am a problem solver!"

"I feel happy, healthy and terrific!"

"I was born to serve!"

"I love my job!"

"I love the clients I am able to serve!"

"I am expecting great things today!"

When you say positive, affirmative and action-focused statements like these – over and over – they eventually begin to sink down into your subconscious mind, which then goes to work to helping your statements come true.

Ladies and gentlemen, you were born to win, you were born to be successful – so talk to yourself in a positive manner and help yourself become the champion you were meant to be!

142 – Get Around the Table

There are definitely some sales professionals reading who sell in their clients' or prospects' homes.

Over the weekend I met with a small group who meet their clients in homes, offices and coffee shops.

Industries that often meet in homes include insurance, direct sales and, of course, real estate.

If you meet your clients or prospects in homes, where are you sitting?

I would recommend you sit around the dining room table if at all possible.

Why?

Because only family and welcome guests sit around the table.

The table usually has the best lighting in the home.

The family is more comfortable sitting around the table.

It gives you space to demo your products or brochures where every-one can see.

Business and family matters are discussed often at the table – so you being there with your ideas, products and services will be seen as an extension of normal conversation.

It's simple, but a great sales idea!

If you are selling in homes, sit around the dining room table if at all possible.

"Everything you've ever wanted is on the other side of fear."

– George Addair

143 – More on the Incredible Power of Focus

Currently I am reading a book called *The Brain Advantage*.

In the book the co-authors cite a study co-sponsored by the University of Illinois and Microsoft.

The study looks at multi-tasking in the workplace.

Now, everyone knows that throughout the day we are called on to do different things at different times AND there are countless interruptions!

- The telephone rings.
- An instant message or text message comes in.
- A co-worker pops in to chat.
- We are distracted by something else we may or may not need to do.

The surprise from the study is that it takes about 15 minutes to get back to work after these seemingly innocent interruptions.

The moral:

Use blocks of uninterrupted focus time to accomplish tasks that really need to be finished fast.

> "There is incredible power in focus, when you FOCUS on it!"
>
> – AL ARGO

144 – Be Flexible!

Flexibility is the key to success in any area of life, especially leadership and sales.

Preparation is the key that allows you to be more flexible. The truth is, the more prepared you are for a sales call, the more flexible you can be on it.

Flexibility then boosts your ability to create rapport. The more flexible you appear to be for your prospects and clients, the easier it becomes for you to establish rapport with them.

In fact, Erika Anderson, author of *Leading So People Will Follow* and Forbes contributor, recently referenced an article from Psychological Science that says that "the people who get the best sales results are those who can flex between introverted and extroverted behavior."

This means you do not always appear to be overly extroverted and do not always exhibit introverted signals either.

What this means to you and me is that we should seek not to mock our prospects, but to mirror them so they are more comfortable around us.

I've always encouraged people attending my seminars to match the speaking rate and mirror the body language of the people they are speaking with.

So, your Super Sales Success Tip for today is simply be flexible! From setting appointments to your speaking style – it pays to be flexible!

> "Don't be afraid to give up the good to go for the great."
>
> – JOHN D. ROCKEFELLER

145 – Do the Right Thing

Your Super Sales Success Tip of the day is: Do the right thing!

This morning I began to read a book entitled *Leading with Honor*. While I'm just getting into it, I can tell the premise is simply that we should "always do the right thing."

Yesterday, I read a story about a prominent person here in the Philippines who "falsified" some receipts. While the amounts were very small, his action was completely wrong and therefore he'll probably be sentenced to six months to two years behind bars. NOT a good trade for $200, is it?

Do the right thing!

In sales, in leadership and in life, we are faced with decisions each day.

And sometimes, we might have an opportunity to cheat others for our benefit.

When you're tempted, resist the temptation and do the right thing!

When you make great decisions like this, I can assure you things will turn out great for you in the long run!

> "Well done is better than well said."
>
> – BENJAMIN FRANKLIN

146 – The 163,000 Pound Phone Bill

Your Super Sales Success Tip for the day is: Rectify mistakes quickly!

For 15 years, Alan and Carolyn had a business deal with a particular cellular company in Europe.

The cellular company provided service for 10 business phones and every month this couple paid around 300-400 pounds (about 500 USD).

And then one day they received a whopping bill for 163,000 pounds. (That's almost a quarter of a million US dollars.)

Of course, the couple knew there was some mistake, so they contacted the company.

The company said they'd fix the problem, but the bills kept coming. And then their phone service was disconnected.

Ladies and gentlemen, this was a business account.

This was an obvious billing mistake.

Yet, the phone company couldn't get it right and kept hounding the couple and threatening legal action.

After seven months of runaround, this couple (who'd been a faithful client for 15 years) finally had to find a new cellular company – and now that it's all over the news, the company finally apologizes and offers them 250 pounds for their "trouble."

Too little – too late?

Your Super Sales Success Tip for today is to rectify mistakes quickly!

"Mistakes are always forgivable, if one has the courage to admit them."

– BRUCE LEE

147 – Persistence Still Pays

Your Super Sales Success Tip for the day is: Persistence still pays!

I have read with keen interest this week about how long JVR (a local Filipino politician) ran for mayor before finally being elected last week – I believe something like 16 years!

And this, ladies and gentlemen, is another example of persistence.

It took Abraham Lincoln 28 years from the time he first attempted to enter American politics until he was elected President.

Have you ever heard of Aaron Levie?

Probably not!

However, Aaron Levie, before he turned 30, was a multimillionaire because of the incredible power of cold calling, persistence and determination.

He is the founder of the cloud storage company Box.

When he first started Box several years ago, no one really knew what cloud computing was – yet today his service is used by 460 of the Fortune 500 companies.

Most of those accounts came about because of persistent cold calling.

Most of his funding came because of persistent cold calling.

Whatever your company, whatever your product or service, be pleasant and be persistent because persistence still pays.

"You just can't beat the person who never gives up."

– BABE RUTH

148 – Compile Compelling Testimonial Letters

I recently asked Nemia Medalle-Corilla, the HRD Manager of General Milling Corporation, to write a testimonial letter for me, and this is what she wrote:

"He was so electrifying and energizing that all the participants were on their toes attentively listening and participating ... The recollection of the learning is high because of Al's unique style of training/facilitating ... You would greatly benefit from Al Argo for your training engagements, hence I highly recommend him."

Doesn't it sound much better coming from her, than it would if I were saying these things about myself.

When you talk about your product or service, you might be considered boasting, but when you showcase a letter from a satisfied client, they are simply saying what your product or service did for them.

Which is more convincing?

Of course, the testimonial letter on your client's letterhead is most convincing!

How come most salespeople don't "bother" to compile testimonial letters?

Your guess is as good as mine!

"It's difficult?" – Not really!

"People don't want to write the letter?" – Most would!

This is a great and underutilized tool to add to your arsenal if you want to double your sales FAST!

Today's Super Sales Success Tip is to compile compelling testimonial letters!

149 – 5 Tips for Compiling and Using Testimonial Letters

In our last tip, we talked about the importance of using testimonial letters. Now, I'd like to share with you five tips for compiling and using great testimonial letters. This is a great way to boost your sales!

1) Ask your best, most satisfied and high-profile clients for a letter.

2) If they are too busy, offer to write the letter for them and let them make any changes or corrections

3) Be specific in terms of product (or service) benefits.

4) Encourage them to write it on their letterhead and email/mail it to you.

5) Showcase the letters in a binder for other potential clients.

When you do these five things you will surely be on your way to Super Sales Success!

> "The successful warrior is the average man, with laser-like focus."
>
> – BRUCE LEE

150 – Remember, Your Customers are Tuned into WIIFM

Your Super Sales Success Tip of the day is to simply remember that your customers and prospects are always tuned into WIIFM.

They are always thinking, asking and dreaming about "what's in it for me?"

You see, they are not buying your product and service for you; they are not buying from you so you can get a higher commission or to help you pay your mortgage.

They are buying your product or service to make it their own.

They are buying it because they want it, desire it or need it.

Your role, as a professional salesperson, is to help them see WHY it is in their best interest to buy from you today!

Maybe it solves a problem!

Maybe it meets a need.

Maybe demand is high, but stock is low.

As you go about your business today, understand your customers, clients and prospects are tuned into WIIFM - they are asking themselves: "What's in it for me?"

"If you can fill the unforgiving minute
With sixty seconds' worth of distance run,
Yours is the Earth and everything that's in it,
And – which is more – you'll be a Man, my son!"

– RUDYARD KIPLING

151 – Act As If

Your Super Sales Success Tip is to act as if!

Act as if it were impossible to fail.

Act as if everyone you are going to meet today will buy.

Act as if you are the greatest salesperson in the world.

Act as if you work for the greatest company in the world and that you are selling the greatest products or services in the world.

Act as if you have unlimited energy and enthusiasm!

Act as if today is the last day of the sales cycle, so you have to get your entire quota sold today – and THEN, do this again tomorrow and the next day!

When you act as if, you'll soon discover that you can do more, be more and sell more than you've ever dreamed possible!

Act as if - and do great things today!

> "Act as if what you do makes a difference. It does."
>
> – WILLIAM JAMES

152 – Enjoy the Journey

Life, leadership and sales can be challenging, complicated and yet very rewarding.

My encouragement for you today is to enjoy, embrace and enhance your journey!

Life, and your occupation, is a gift – enjoy your life and the opportunity you've been given.

You will undoubtedly enjoy your life and even your job more if you will make the decision to embrace it – I mean really embrace each and every day with gusto and enthusiasm!

And last, but not least, you know that I refer to my name AL as an acronym for "Always Learning." This again is a reminder that we, indeed, need to enhance our journey.

Don't settle for mediocrity!

Don't settle for average!

Don't settle for "no one in my family has done it, so I can't either."

Instead, focus on learning, development, and growing in your personal and professional life.

My challenge for you today is to enjoy, embrace and enhance your journey – because when you get the journey right, you'll get the destination right!

"Enjoy, embrace and enhance the journey! If you get the journey right, you'll get the destination right!"

– AL ARGO

153 – Be Happy

Your Super Sales Success Tip of the day is: Be happy!

Happiness IS NOT something to pursue, it's something to BE!

As Abraham Lincoln said, "Most people are about as happy as they make up their minds to be."

Again, we don't pursue happiness – we pursue positive impact!

We pursue making a difference for our clients, families, friends and neighbors.

So if you're not happy today, GET Happy!

According to research, happy people are healthier people.

Happy people sell more!

Happy people earn more!

Happy people are more productive!

Happy people have more fun!

Happy people bring more joy to others!

Hey, it's a beautiful day – my challenge to you today is "Don't worry - be happy!"

"Most people are about as happy as they make up their minds to be."

– ABRAHAM LINCOLN

154 – Give Back

Your Super Sales Success Tip of the day is: Give back!

I'd like to personally shout out to and THANK all the players, parents, volunteers, coaches and refs who've helped out in Upward Sports across Asia.

We believe everyone is a VIP and every child is a champion and made in the image of God.

All of our leaders, coaches and referees are volunteers, which brings me to the Super Sales Success tip of the day – Give Back!

Ed, owner of Franzy Hair Salons, gave back as a parent volunteer through Upward.

Albert, CEO of SpellDial, gave back as a coach through Upward.

Binky over at Island Souvenirs gave back as a special assistant through Upward.

These three, along with countless others like Coli, Anisha, BamShack, DonDon and April, Bado, Mark, Simeon, John, Shawn, Jazel, Jerome, Sharon, and Rainier among even others, made the decision to volunteer for the Upward Sports league as I am writing this book.

Hey, these volunteers made it possible for the children in their community to learn more about soccer, enjoy league play and grow in character development in the inaugural Upward Sports Soccer League in their city.

My challenge for you is to find a charity, find a cause and volunteer! GIVE BACK!

155 – See Yourself Successful

Today's Super Sales Success Tip is to see yourself successful!

If you don't see it in your mind first, it's much more difficult in real life.

Let me explain:

Several weeks ago, in the coffee shop my wife and I are blessed to help run, a new acquaintance of ours received a phone call from a prospective employer.

Her negative thinking led her to indicate she really did not want to work for the company.

After the phone call, I asked her if she wanted the job.

"Of course!" she exclaimed.

"Then why didn't you let them offer you the position," I asked.

She NEVER saw herself as successful, so in order to avoid a perceived "rejection," she verbally told them she did not really want to work for them.

I would not have believed this if I had not heard it with my own ears.

But you should do the opposite of what our friend did – you should see yourself as wildly successful!

See yourself as making the sell.

See yourself as getting the promotion.

See yourself as winning the marathon you have signed up for.

See yourself as reaching your wildest and most ambitious goals.

See it in your mind first, see yourself working towards the big goal and see yourself achieving the big goal – then go accomplish your wildest dreams today!

156 – Keep Testing Your Limits

I recently had the opportunity to watch Man of Steel, a great movie in the Superman franchise.

In the movie, Jor-El, Superman's father, is quoted as saying, "Keep testing your limits!"

This is a great tip as we come to the end of the Super Sales Success Tips.

Keep testing your limits!

Seek to see more clients and prospects today than you have ever seen.

Seek to sell more today than you have ever sold.

Seek to get more referrals today than you have ever received.

Keep testing your limits, and believe that your records were meant to be broken by you!

Keep testing your limits and you'll see that you can sell more, and in fact you can achieve more, than you've ever dreamed possible.

"Keep testing your limits!"

– Jor-El

157 – Don't Quit

This poem was printed inside the last page of my sales manual while I was in college. I trust it reminds you to stay focused, work hard, work smart and never quit!

"Don't Quit"

"When things go wrong, as they sometimes will,
When the road you're trudging seems all uphill,
When the funds are low and the debts are high,
And you want to smile, but you have to sigh,
When care is pressing you down a bit,
Rest, if you must, but don't you quit.
Life is queer with its twists and turns,
As every one of us sometimes learns,
And many a failure turns about,
When he might have won had he stuck it out;
Don't give up though the pace seems slow–
You may succeed with another blow.
Often the goal is nearer than,
It seems to a faint and faltering man,
Often the struggler has given up,
When he might have captured the victor's cup,
And he learned too late when the night slipped down,
How close he was to the golden crown.
Success is failure turned inside out–
The silver tint of the clouds of doubt,

And you never can tell how close you are,
It may be near when it seems so far,
So stick to the fight when you're hardest hit–
It's when things seem worst that you must not quit."

158 – Read Like Your Sales Depends on It

Your Super Sales Success Tip of the day is: Read like your sales depend on it – when you read like your sales depends on it, your closing ratio, your productivity and then your income are sure to increase dramatically.

In fact, when I was first starting out in sales, one book I read led to me tripling my sales in about three months.

And that will be the last book I tell you about in this Super Sales Success Tip.

Here are some great books you should definitely check out:

- *The Bible* – Most great personal and professional growth ideas stem from Biblical thoughts
- *The Greatest Salesman in the World* by Og Mandino
- *Life is Tremendous* by Charles "Tremendous" Jones
- *The Ultimate Sales Machine* by Chet Holmes
- *Think & Grow Rich* by Napoleon Hill
- *Walking, Living, Learning* by Al Argo
- *Wake Up & Shine* by Al Argo
- Any book by John Maxwell
- Any book by Brian Tracy
- Any book by Jeffrey Gitomer
- Any book by Tom Hopkins

And the book that helped me triple my sales in just three months is:

Secrets of Closing the Sale by Zig Ziglar.

Read anything you can by Zig Ziglar and the other authors I have mentioned and Super Sales Success really can be yours!

One of my mentors, Charles "Tremendous" Jones, once said, "You and I are the same today as we will be five years from now, except for two things: The people you meet and the books you read!"

Read like your sales depend on it, and watch your sales soar!

"Change before you have to."
— JACK WELCH

159 – See Each Person as a 10

I learned this tip from John Maxwell, the influential leadership guru and author of The 21 Irrefutable Laws of Leadership and countless other leadership and personal development books.

Every time you see a person, put a 10 on their head! What I mean is, see the potential that they represent!

Do this with your clients, prospects, co-workers, friends and family members.

This is great advice for several reasons:

1) People often live up to the expectations that are placed on them – when you expect people to perform at a higher level, often they sense it and live up to your expectations. It's better to have high expectations and be a little short than to have lower expectations and end up being mediocre.

2) The Mirror Principle – If you see others as a 10, you will also begin to truly see yourself as a 10. Your attitudes and actions are contagious – if you see others as happy, you will become even happier. If you see others as productive, you can become even more productive. Make sense?

Expect the best from yourself and others and see everyone you meet as a 10 and full of unlimited potential!

> "We herd sheep, we drive cattle, we lead people.
> Lead me, follow me, or get out of my way."
>
> – GEORGE S. PATTON

160 – Momentum

You've reached the very last tip of this entire book! My question for you today is, "How is your momentum?"

Peg Wood said, "Commitment is the igniter of momentum."

Momentum is defined as your force of movement toward a worthwhile goal.

Goals can never be achieved without action and movement toward your goal.

If we were on a great mountain covered with snow and were to roll a ball of snow down the mountain, the ball would start slowly, but as it rolled and rolled down the hill it would get bigger and bigger and faster and faster as it gained momentum.

That's how your goals are – the more you work hard and smart toward your goals, the more successful you will be!

Momentum is achieved by doing something every day that can help you reach your biggest, wildest goals.

I encourage people to always ask the question, WCIDT?

Which again stands for "What can I do today to achieve my goals?"

Consistent and persistent work toward your goals helps you to maintain, sustain and eventually propel your momentum!

In the morning, people often drink a cup of Joe – but today, I am encouraging you to serve yourself some 'Mo – meaning "serve yourself some momentum!"

Do something today, and every day, to stay on course to reaching your wildest hopes, dreams and goals!

Now go make it a great day for your clients and your future because Super Sales Success belongs to YOU!

"Our greatest weakness lies in giving up. The most certain way to succeed is always to try just one more time."

– THOMAS EDISON

Like what you've read? Your positive review on Amazon, Goodreads or Audible will help others discover *160 Super Sales Success Tips* as well! Thanks in advance!

Don't forget to check out *Walking, Living, Learning! An Adventure in Personal & Professional Development & Wake Up & Shine: 7 Morning Habits that Guarantee Daily Success & Significance.*

Need a speaker?
E-mail Al Argo at argoglobal@gmail.com

www.ingramcontent.com/pod-product-compliance
Lightning Source LLC
Chambersburg PA
CBHW051511170526
45166CB00001B/478